The Farmers Market Cookbook

THE FARMERS MARKET COOKBOOK

by Fran Jurga Garvan

Illustrated by W. David Powell

THE HARVARD COMMON PRESS
Harvard, Massachusetts

The Harvard Common Press
The Common, Harvard, Massachusetts 01451

Printed in the United States of America.

Library of Congress Cataloguing in Publication Data

Garvan, Fran Jurga
    The farmers market cookbook.

    Includes index.
      1. Cookery.   2. Farm produce—United States—Marketing.
I. Title.
TX715.G236   1982   641.5   82-11768
ISBN 0-916782-29-8
ISBN 0-916782-30-1 (pbk.)

Cover and illustrations by W. David Powell

10 9 8 7 6 5 4 3 2 1

This one's for you, Steve.

ACKNOWLEDGEMENTS

Many people put time and energy into helping me on this project, and I would like to thank them in print. Thanks to Margaret Hanni, Kathy Schloff, Alicia Jenks, JoJo Levasseur, Caddie Johannsen, Swaz, Jacque, Sofian, and all the other great chefs of Vermont who guided me through this experience; thanks to Alden Miller of the Worcester County Extension Service for his resources and enthusiasm for farmers markets; thanks to the Division of Food and Agriculture of the states of Massachusetts and Maine; thanks to Amy Brown and Kathleen Cushman for having patience and belief in this book; thanks to my parents for their recipes and rhubarb (and lots more); thanks to Bruce Shaw for holding pies in his lap; and thanks to the farmers, for coming to market.

CONTENTS

Ain't nobody here hungry?

—Vendor's cry at Haymarket, Boston

INTRODUCTION

AMERICANS have finally woken up. The great supermarket rebellion came and went during the seventies, leaving behind in its wake a new consciousness of American agriculture, a new appreciation for fresh foods, and an organized network of farmers markets across the country.

Farmers markets are nothing new. In fact, the idea is one of the oldest ones around. When subsistence farming blossomed with agricultural advances and the first farmer sold his extra produce to a neighbor, the system was born. Around the world a tradition that began in the Dark Ages, and maybe before, became a basis for the social, religious, and economic structures of hamlets, villages, and cities. And, in most, the tradition thrives still, uninterrupted by changes in almost every other facet of life.

In some cultures, open air markets are the only source of food. In others, they are a supplement to larger dealers. But always farmers markets are recognized as a vital part of the economy and a traditional social activity, particularly in countries where food storage and transportation are difficult.

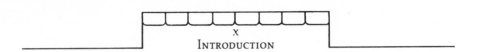

In France open air markets are fiercely preserved, for that country has seen the writing on the wall; if local farmers are not encouraged to keep up their growing and selling cycles, France will have to depend on other governments to supply food. The French people do not want that. Instead, the French want to maintain a balance between agriculture and industry. In short, they want to be affluent enough to afford their foie gras, but they realize that their earnings would be of less value without their native food culture.

France has strict controls on imported food, particularly fresh produce. Even the fruits imported from French territories like Martinique and Guadalupe can only be offered in French markets during the periods when native fruits of the same species are unavailable.

America, on the other hand, does not exert these types of controls. A quick wheel through a supermarket in any U.S. city will verify that. Produce from South America, Africa, and Asia is offered alongside native produce; and sometimes, sadly, native produce is nowhere in sight. The American food picture is a complex one, and agricultural crops have become an important part of trade negotiations and treaties. As a result Americans have grown accustomed to having fresh fruits and vegetables, regardless of frosts, floods, and Med flies. If one source can't supply us, another can. And most people never know the origin of their food anyway.

Farmers markets are not designed to beat this system. They are intended to supplement the system by offering an alternative to supermarket produce and packaging. Farmers markets benefit the consumer and the seller.

What's a farmers market? A farmers market can be anything from a group of local gardeners selling their extra zucchini out of the back of station wagons to a huge indoor arena of food sellers and dealers that attracts thousands of customers a day. Markets fall into every category for rural and urban sites, and the only thing that they all have in common is a clientele seeking fresh, wholesome food. The vendors may be the growers themselves or they may be professional vendors who resell produce bought at wholesale markets. They may be concerned organic farmers or wisecracking wheeler-dealers. The buyers choose their vendors.

In Los Angeles, the Farmers Market attracts about 20,000 people a day, everyone from the elderly to restaurant chefs. The huge indoor facility is a privately owned and operated circus of all kinds of food. Most of the 160 vendors sell produce, but there are tempting concessioners selling everything from tacos to ice cream.

The booths at the Farmers Market in Los Angeles are operated on 30-day leases, but some vendors have thousands of dollars invested in their spaces. They have no fear of the market folding. Competition is fierce; and the food offered is of the highest quality. Buyers come back, sometimes daily, to their favorite vendors. A trip to the Los Angeles Farmers Market is a trip to an ancient traditional market that has gone slightly mad with abundance and gourmet delight. Everything is there that you have always dreamed of, but fresher, lusher, and a little bit cheaper.

No matter what size a farmers market is, acceptance by the public seems to be universal. People like to shop at farmers markets and they will, if they have access and time.

Access and time are two big problems with farmers markets. Supermarkets are always open, and there's always a parking space waiting. It may be easier to sweep through a Safeway and get all of one's produce, meat, and groceries at once. Some people don't have time to go to different locations or are busy on the days when farmers markets are open. But everyone should try to shop at a farmers market when the opportunity arises.

For consumers, farmers markets are the best way to purchase food. One only has to go once to the Eastern Market in Detroit, Michigan to understand why. On a Saturday morning, there may be as many as 40,000 people there picking out their week's food. Many restaurant chefs and caterers are in the crowd, too. The food is fresher—often picked the same day, and prices are lower than the supermarkets'. The buyer can talk to the vendor about the origin of the food. In many cases, the vendor *is* the grower, or a family member. Farmers markets support local and regional farmers and

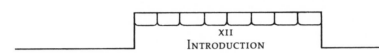

help to preserve and promote agriculture in the area. New York City's famous Greenmarket attracts farmers from as far as 200 miles away. They know that they can sell their fruit and vegetables, and many advertise the fact that their prices are below supermarkets'. The crowds keep coming.

How does the consumer get the most out of a farmers market? First of all, *know your eating habits.* Don't go unprepared. This cookbook is designed to give you some ideas for foods available at farmers markets. Unless otherwise indicated, each recipe serves 4 to 6 people. Pick out a recipe and buy the ingredients while you're out; don't buy three pounds of fiddleheads and try to think of a way to cook them when you get home. Plan ahead.

Make a list of what you would like to buy. Some things may not be available or may be too expensive. I waited months for the California oranges to come in this winter, but when they came, it was worth the wait. Include non-produce items on your list. If the market doesn't sell eggs and dairy products, ask where you can get them fresh. Also, on your list, write the quantities that you will need. That will keep you from overbuying.

Think about quality. If fruit is to be used in a fruit bowl, it should be beautiful and top quality. If you are making jelly, ask for second quality. Remember that the nutritional value of produce is the same, regardless of what it looks like, unless it is unripe or overripe.

Scout out the whole market before you buy. At a good market, if you want asparagus you'll be able to find spears of all shapes and diameters, wild and domesticated, in shades of green, purple, and white. Don't buy from the first vendor unless you're in a big hurry. Check out the other stalls' prices and quality first.

Get to know a few vendors. If you buy from them regularly, they will start to know you too. Your repeat business will help stabilize the market. Your vendors will know what you like and keep your needs in mind.

Ask a lot of questions. Don't hesitate to ask what something is or how to clean or cook it. If the fish man isn't busy, ask him to point out

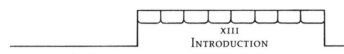

the different types of filets. Ask if a certain type of fish is apt to be bony, and how long it will stay fresh in the refrigerator. Ask where the food came from. Was it grown with pesticides? You'll never know the answers unless you ask, and the vendors will respect you for asking.

Don't poke the merchandise. It's hard not to, but you really won't be able to tell much with your thumb stuck through an eggplant. Damaged produce costs money. Just pick a specimen up—just one will do. Hold it in your hand and check for blemishes, texture, weight, and firmness. And when it comes to corn, be careful. The temptation is overwhelming to strip each ear, but don't. Ask the variety and get to know how different kinds fill out. Some become plump and others stay slim, even when fully ripe. Learn to feel the perfect ear and always buy a few extra, just in case. If there is one thing that will drive a vendor into a frenzy, it is corn stripping. I'm a reformed corn stripper myself. I may buy a dozen ears, strip them in the car, and go back for two more. It's the luck of the draw.

Know quantities. Most foods are sold by the pound, and at some stands there may be a pound minimum. Keep that in mind as you scout the market. I would much rather buy the bunch or dozen or even by dry volume than by weight, but sometimes there's no choice. Bags are a help here. Bags come in sizes that are approximately equal to dry volume measure when full. Especially at harvest time, keep these figures in mind:

1 quart = 1 #2 bag
2½ quarts = 1 lunch-size bag
1 gallon = 1 #8 bag
1 peck = 1 #20 bag
1 bushel = 4 #20 bags

And remember: A bushel of *anything* is a lot.

Protect your purchases. Bring a market basket with you or get a double-lined department store shopping bag. Pack the heaviest items, like corn, zucchini, and melons, on the bottom. Bring some extra plastic bags with you to double wrap delicate fruits or cheeses. Vendors usually supply brown bags, but they will appreciate it if you bring your own. If you're not going home directly, put a cooler in the back of your car and move the most perishable produce there. My pasta-making vendor wraps the bags of pasta in newspaper if it's hot out or if I have other errands. Wet the paper to protect leafy spinach and lettuce. As the water evaporates, it will cool the vegetables.

Discuss prices—don't bargain. If you expect rock-bottom prices, you're likely to get rock-bottom quality and service. Don't forget that vendors have invested considerable effort and expense in growing or purchasing the food, building a stand, renting space, and hiring help. Don't expect to find super bargains at the end of the day either. Sometimes the price will go down but some vendors will be sold out. Is it worth a few pennies to have food that sat out all day?

Successful shopping at the farmers market doesn't take an education. These tips will help you make the most of the market near where you live. But it will take many trips before you can really operate at peak efficiency, though even in the beginning, you're ahead. You're shopping at the farmers market and getting the best food at the best prices. And that's a good start.

Quality and Freshness Characteristics for Selected Fresh Fruits and Vegetables

Item	Desired Characteristics
Apples	Colorful, uniform, bruise-free
Apricots	Plump, firm
Artichokes	Bright color, firm
Asparagus	Wilt-free, uniform
Avocados	Smoothness, bruise-free
Bananas	Uniform, mold-free, bright color
Beans, snap	Crisp, uniform immature
Beans, lima	Clean, well-filled, dark green
Beets	Small, smooth, firm
Berries	Bright, clean, plump
Broccoli	Closed buds, clean, dark green
Brussel sprouts	Hard, clean, compact
Cabbage	Hard, heavy, bright color
Carrots	Firm, uniform, well-colored
Cauliflower	White, clean, compact curd
Celery	Medium size, crisp, colorful
Cherries	Bright, plump
Collards	Fresh, immature, colorful
Corn	Bright, plump, milky kernels
Cranberries	High lustre, firm, plump
Cucumbers	Green, well-shaped, firm
Dates	Golden brown, slightly moist
Eggplant	Heavy, rich color, scar free
Endive-escarole	Fresh, immature, colorful
Figs	Fairly soft, uniform
Grapefruit	Springy touch, heavy
Grapes	Plump, mature, fresh
Kale	Fresh, immature, colorful
Leeks	Fresh, uniform, clean

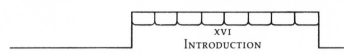
Item	Desired Characteristics
Lemons	Bright, heavy, fine texture
Lettuce	Clean, crisp, tender
Melons	Mature, fine texture, sweet aroma
Mushrooms	Clean, wilt-free, light color
Nectarines	Plump, well-colored, firm
Onions, dry	Hard, bright, dry
Onions, green	Green, fresh, clean, uniform
Parsnips	Smooth, clean, medium size
Peaches	Bright, fresh, yellow background
Peas	Tender, young, sweet
Pears	Firm, unbroken skin, wilt-free
Peppers	Fresh, green color, firm
Persimmons	Resemble plump, ripe tomato
Plums, prunes	Full colored, plump, slightly soft
Potatoes	Smooth, sound, firm
Pumpkins	Hard, blemish free
Radishes	Mild, bright, smooth
Rhubarb	Crisp, bright, stout
Spinach	Fresh, immature, colorful
Squash, summer	Crisp, heavy, tender
Squash, winter	Hard, blemish free
Sweet potatoes	Bright, solid, well-shaped
Tomatoes, unripe	Hard, green
Tomatoes, ripe	Plump, bruise-free, firm, uniform color
Turnips	Heavy, smooth, firm
Watermelons	Mature, well-shaped

JANUARY

FOOD STORAGE

Need a good New Year's Resolution? How about vowing to organize your food storage system once and for all? January is the perfect time to go through your cabinets, root cellar, and freezer and take stock of what you have, what you don't have, what you have too much of, what you don't have enough of, and what you're going to do about it.

Everything in this cookbook is designed with a well-stocked kitchen in mind. The best place to start organizing your social life is right in the middle of your kitchen, so now might be a good time to evaluate both your social and your cooking lives.

There's no doubt about it: one way to keep your friends happy is to feed them. Friends have a peculiar habit of dropping by on Sunday evenings or after midnight, long after the stores are closed. From out of nothing, the omelet was born, and you can entertain your friends and treat them to a delicious meal if you keep your food supply at a reasonable level. I am not recommending an overflowing larder. Food does not have an indefinite shelf life, as it sometimes seems. And no matter how good a deal it sounds like to buy a grocery cart full of anchovy filets, the sad truth is that they will sit on your shelf forever. The money is much better invested in something you will eat.

By organizing your shelves, refrigerator, and long-term storage area by categories, you will save yourself time and frustration when you need to whip up a meal in a hurry. I've made up the following list of things that you should have on hand at all times, and you can use it as a check list.

When it comes to storing canned goods, think first. If you have plenty of shelf area, label the shelves by seasons and years (use by fall 1987; use by spring 1988, etc.). Place goods on the shelves relevant to their life expectancy when you bring them home from the store. This will prevent you from frivolously eating something when something else is perishable, and about to expire. Nobody likes to throw food away.

A CUPBOARD INVENTORY

Close to cooking area

Oils
Olive oil
Blended oil
Peanut oil
Safflower oil
Corn oil
Lard or shortening
Unsalted butter
   at room temperature

Sauces
Soy or Tamari
Worcestershire
Bouillon: beef and chicken
Tabasco or salsa

Spices
Cinnamon
Nutmeg
Allspice
Basil
Thyme
Oregano
Garlic (in closed container)
Bay leaves
Tarragon
Marjoram
Hungarian paprika
Rosemary
Ginger (in closed container)
Cloves, whole and ground
Crushed red pepper

Cayenne
White pepper
Cumin
Chili powder
Cream of tartar
Alum
Herbed salt
Sea salt

For Baking
Vanilla extract
Almond extract
Baking soda
Baking powder
Honey

In Cool, Dry Storage Area

Pasta and Rices
Vermicelli
Capellini
Linguini
Elbows
Egg noodles
Variety of spinach pastas
   or other flavored pastas
Long-grain brown rice
Packaged rice pilaf
Wild rice

Legumes
Dried lentils
Dried pinto beans
Dried split peas
Canned kidney beans
Couscous
Kasha

Baking Needs
Unbleached white flour
Whole wheat pastry flour
Cornmeal
Masa harina
Dark brown sugar
Light brown sugar
Turbanado sugar
White sugar
Confectioners sugar
Corn syrup (light and dark)
Unsweetened chocolate
Semisweet chocolate
Semisweet chocolate chips
Tapioca
Unsweetened gelatin
Salt
Cornstarch

Cereal Products
Oatmeal
Granola

Miscellaneous
Peanut butter
Miscellaneous crackers
Coconut
Dry milk
Cans of evaporated milk
Tea bags
Coffee beans
Cocoa

A CUPBOARD INVENTORY, *continued*

In a Cool, Distant Area

Perishable
10 pounds potatoes
10 pounds yellow onions
2 pounds red onions
Winter squash
Sugar pumpkins
Winter apples
Beets and carrots in soil

Canned
Chicken and beef stocks
Miscellaneous soups
Whole imported tomatoes
Stewed tomatoes
Tomato paste
Pizza sauce
Anchovies
Smoked baby clams

Smoked oysters
Black olives
Clam juice
Clams, minced
Tuna
Canned spinach
Mayonnaise-unopened
Tomato juice

In the Refrigerator

Refrigerator/Freezer
Two trays of ice cubes
Two pounds
    of unsweetened butter
Loaf of bread
Individual snacks
Juices

Top shelf
Soft drinks and juices
Leftover wines for cooking
Bottle of lemon juice
Whole milk
Small container buttermilk

Second shelf
Sour cream
Unflavored yogurt
Cottage cheese
Ricotta
Light cream
Eggs
Half-dozen hard-boiled eggs
Cheddar cheese
Roquefort cheese
Munster cheese
Swiss cheese
Deli meats

Third shelf
Imported mustard in crock
Jar of mustard
Ketchup
Mayonnaise
Miscellaneous jellies and jams
Green olives
Black olives
Herring
Yeast
Raisins
Tahini
Steak sauce

Vegetable/Fruit bin
Mushrooms
Tomatoes
Lettuce
Spinach
Broccoli, cabbage or cauliflower
Green beans or peas
Scallions or leeks
Zucchini or yellow squash
Oranges or apples
Grapefruit or melon
Carrots
Celery
Lemons and limes

SHELF LIFE OF FOOD

Discard after six months of storage

Mayonnaise or commercially prepared
salad dressings
Coffee
Crackers and cookies
Open containers of flour
Open containers of dried fruit and raisins
Open containers of ground spices
Open containers of dried milk
Peanut butter
Open containers of processed sugars
Ketchup

Discard after one year of storage

Maple syrup
Honey
Chocolate of all types
Oils and shortenings
Jellies and jams
Canned tomato products
Cereals and grains
Baking needs
Canned fruits
Canned juices
Condensed soups
Whole spices
Evaporated milk
Nuts
Dried lentils and beans
Canned vegetables
Canned fish or meat

Discard after two years of storage

White sugar
Pasta
Rice

WOODSTOCK LENTIL SOUP

Begin this recipe early in the morning to get most of the work out of the way before dinner. First, wash and clean the spinach, leaving it to dry on paper towels.

Cook the lentils in the beef broth for 20 to 30 minutes until they are swollen and tender. Make sure that the pot has a tight-fitting cover, and try not to peek at them. When the lentils are done, just leave them in the pot to soak until you are ready to cook the rest of the recipe.

When ready, sauté the onion and the garlic in the oil until they are soft. Do not let them brown. Put the lentils on low heat; they should just simmer.

Heat the tomatoes in a saucepan over medium heat. When they are hot, add the spinach. Stir the spinach as it cooks until it turns the characteristic dark green color and gets soft. Make sure that the spinach is evenly distributed through the tomatoes. If your leaves are huge or the spinach sticks together in globs, put the tomato-spinach mixture in a blender and blend on medium speed until smooth.

Add the spinach-tomato mixture to the lentils and stir well so that everything gets nicely mixed together. Pour in the sherry (you can be more generous if you like a richly flavored soup) and add salt and pepper. Cover the pan and cook everything together for about 15 minutes. Just before serving time, check the consistency. If you like a thin soup, add water or a mixture of water and beef broth. To thicken the soup, cook longer.

Pour or ladle the soup into ovenproof soup bowls. Top with shredded or grated Gruyere (about 2 tablespoons per bowl) and place in a preheated oven at 400°. When cheese is melted, remove quickly from oven and serve. Garnish cheese topping with a sprig of fresh parsley, and serve a wedge of lemon on the side.

1 cup dry lentils
3 tablespoons blended oil, La
  Spagnola brand
4 cups beef broth
1 pound spinach, washed and
  trimmed
1 onion, choped finely
1 clove minced garlic
1 2-pound can peeled
  tomatoes
2 tablespoons dry sherry
Salt and pepper to taste
Shredded Gruyere cheese
  (about ½ cup or so)

ONION SOUP PARMESAN

Look for the big round 4-inch diameter onions in your travels through the market. Two will probably be enough, but if you are feeding a crowd or want to have reserves of soup, get three or even four.

Peel the onions and slice them into thin rounds. Poke the onions in the center of the slices to transform them into onion rings. You may wish to cut the rings in two if they are too big. With smaller onions, you can leave them whole.

Melt the butter in the base of a large kettle, preferably the Dutch oven sort. Sauté the onion in the butter until it gets soft. Do not let it brown. Stir the onion slices as they cook. You will feel them getting more tender as you stir. Keep the flame low and stir constantly so that the onions cook very slowly. When the onions are a golden yellow, they're ready.

Sprinkle the flour over the onions. If the onions are dry, melt more butter, and add it before the flour. Add more than two tablespoons of flour if that doesn't seem to be enough for the big onions. Continue to stir until all the onions are coated with flour and the mixture is thick. Then slowly add the chicken broth, stirring as you pour.

Keep stirring until the whole mixture begins to bubble and boil. Then lower the heat and let the soup simmer for about 15 minutes with a cover on to insure the heat.

Just before you are ready to serve, pour in the wine and remove the lid. You can turn up the heat a little bit (it's cheating, but it works) to insure even heating, but be sure to remove the cover and leave it off. While the soup is heating, prepare the soup bowls.

Place a piece of toasted French bread, crust removed, in the bottom of each dish. Grate enough fresh

2-3 very large mild onions
¼ cup unsalted butter
2 tablespoons flour
1 quart chicken broth
2 cups dry red wine
One ½" slice of toasted
    French bread per serving
2 tablespoons grated fresh
    Parmesan per serving

ONION SOUP, *continued*

Parmesan in each dish to the taste of your guests; if they're a cheese-loving crowd, go ahead and be liberal with the cheese. They'll love it.

Pour the soup into the bowls and top with the grated Parmesan. If the soup is hot, it will melt the Parmesan on contact. If the Parmesan rebels and stays whole, run the soup bowls under the broiler quickly (10 seconds or so) but make sure that the dishes are ovenproof.

WHAT CAN YOU SELL OR BUY AT A FARMERS MARKET?

Traditional

Fresh fruits and vegetables
Native produce
Ethnic/regional specialties
Herbs
Meats

Non-traditional

Honey or maple syrup
Preserves, jams, jellies, and other
    homemade specialties
House and herb plants
Farm-fresh eggs
Baked goods or wholesale odd lots
Prepared pie fillings or food sauces,
salad dressings
Herb products
Ciders and juices
Homemade ice cream

Experimental

Handicrafts
Puppies and kittens
Poultry
Feed grain
Dried beans and nuts
Fresh homemade pasta

REFRIED BEANS

Put the beans in a heavy saucepan with 4 cups of water. Put a tight-fitting lid on the pan and heat the beans to a boil. Reduce heat and simmer the beans for at least 2 hours. The beans will break open and be soft to the touch when they are ready. Watch out that the water doesn't boil away; add more if it is getting low, but not more than 1 inch.

Heat the olive oil in a frying pan, and fry the garlic pieces. Then add beans by the spoonful from the bean pot. Mash them down into the corners of the frying pan. If the beans get dry, add some water to the middle of the pan. Allow the edges to get a little crusty. Keep pan on low heat as the beans cook. When beans become a solid mass with a good crust, add some water to the center of the bean mass. Add cumin and chili powder to taste. One good measure is to lean over the pan, and inhale the vapors as you add the spice. When the unique odor of the spice hits your nostrils, you probably have added enough.

Pour the diced tomatoes into the center of the pan. Then fold the bean mass over so that the tomato is sealed inside, although somewhat mashed. Serve in a shallow bowl or use as a filling.

1 *pound dry pinto beans*
2 *tablespoons olive oil*
1 *clove of garlic, minced*
1 *tablespoon each: cumin, chili powder, and oregano*
1 *cup diced tomato*

GOLD RUSH BEAN ROLLS

I would walk all the way to Nashville, Tennessee for one of these bean rolls if I didn't have the recipe. This is *the* recipe for bean rolls from the famous Gold Rush saloon in Nashville. When the Gold Rush chef Mitch Williams, a transplanted Texan, married my wonderful friend Katina, I actually got to meet the man behind the legendary bean roll. When I decided to start this book and began to collect recipes, Mitch was my first phone call. If this book has done nothing else, it has brought me closer to true happiness by being able to make Gold Rush bean rolls in the comfort of my home. I'll miss Nashville.

One note: there is an extra step in here, the dry fry step. You can leave it out and still have wonderful bean rolls. The choice is yours.

Begin by laying out an 8-inch flour tortilla on a cutting board in front of you. Gather all the rest of your ingredients around the cutting board in a kind of semicircle, so that nothing is out of arm's reach.

Spread a spoonful of hot, sizzling refried beans in the middle of the tortilla. Top the beans with a handful of well-shredded Monterey Jack cheese. (Cheddar will do if you can't get Monterey Jack.) Make sure that the cheese is well shredded on the small side of a cheese grater, so that it will melt easily.

On top of the cheese, sprinkle onions and tomatoes. Roll up the tortilla carefully, folding the ends in toward the center.

Lift the tortilla carefully, and using a long spatula, place the tortilla in a large skillet or omelet pan. Dry fry until it is brown on each side and the cheese starts to ooze out the edges. Over medium heat, it should take about five minutes to reach this stage.

Now, using the spatula again, lift the tortilla out

Per tortilla:
1 flour tortilla
½ cup refried beans
½ cup shredded Monterey Jack cheese
1 tablespoon diced onion
2 tablespoons diced tomato
¼ cup hot sauce
Hard-boiled eggs and sour cream for garnish

GOLD RUSH BEAN ROLLS, *continued*

of the frying pan and place it in an ovenproof pan that is lined with aluminum foil for easy cleanup. Cover it with your favorite hot sauce and more grated cheese.

Run the tortilla under the broiler until the cheese on top melts and runs over the edges. Pull out of the broiler immediately and transfer gently to a plate.

If necessary, add more hot sauce (heated), and garnish with pickled jalapeno and carrot slices, hard-boiled egg quarters, and a dollop of sour cream. Serve immediately.

BLACK OLIVE SALAD

Rinse the olives well and drain in a colander. Shake to remove any water inside the olives. Transfer olives to a bowl, and pour wine vinegar and oil over them. Sprinkle paprika and garlic on top and fold over with a wooden spoon until the seasonings are well mixed. Cover with plastic wrap and chill in refrigerator for a few hours.

Before serving time, remove olives from refrigerator. Add drained pimento and fold in. Arrange the olives and pimento on the serving dish you plan to use, and arrange quarter wedges of hard-boiled egg around or among the olives. Serve bread on the side or as croutons.

2 *cups pitted black olives*
¼ *cup olive oil*
¼ *cup red wine vinegar*
2 *teaspoons sweet paprika*
2 *cloves garlic, minced*
1 *can pimento, drained*
4 *hard-boiled eggs, chilled*
6 *slices of dark rye bread or*
   pumpernickel

IT'S A HIT CHILI

Sauté the onion, green pepper, garlic, and sausage in the oil until the sausage is well browned on all sides. Slit the sausage skins and throw them away. Next break up the sausage meat with a fork, and mix well with the onions and peppers.

Drain off any excess fat. Put beef in the pan with onions, peppers, and sausage meat and turn up the heat a bit. Stir as you cook the beef. When beef is almost brown, pour 1 cup of water over it. Add chili powder and cumin to the water-soaked meat. Sprinkle spices liberally on top of water. Then increase heat to high, and stir constantly as water evaporates and beef browns.

When all the water is gone, add tomatoes, and simmer for about 20 minutes. Then add beans and stir; cook for about 15 minutes. If mixture is too liquid, add tomato paste to soak up moisture.

A few minutes before serving, add jalapeno relish a teaspoon at a time. If you are shy of very hot food, serve the jalapeno relish in a dish for those who like their chili hot. The chili will be plenty spicy without the relish.

Serve cornbread on the side. If somebody bites into a solid piece of jalapeno, tell him to take a quick bite of the bread. It will help a lot more than a gulp of water.

3 *pounds lean ground beef*
2 *green peppers, chopped*
2 *medium onions, chopped*
1 *pound mild Italian sausage*
2 *cloves garlic*
¼ *cup olive oil*
3 *large cans of stewed*
   tomatoes
Chili powder, to taste
Equal amount of cumin
2 *pounds soaked or canned*
   pinto beans
1 *can tomato paste*
Jalapeno relish to taste
Cornbread

MARINATED BLACK OLIVES

Try to buy black olives in an Italian market or at least in the deli section of a supermarket. If all else fails, buy two cans of imported black olives.

Combine: black olives (rinsed and drained), olive oil, red wine vinegar, chopped scallions or shallots, and garlic. Sprinkle paprika over all and marinate at room temperature for 6 or more hours. Delicious served with rye bread and cream cheese.

3 cups pitted black olives
½ cup olive oil
½ cup red wine vinegar
2 tablespoons chopped scallions or shallots
2 garlic cloves
Paprika

COSMIC CAULIFLOWER: THE LEGEND

I was snowbound once with "Cosmic Mike," a genuine friend of mine. There were, as I remember, four of us in the farmhouse that day. The snow was coming down in blankets, and we sat around the kitchen quite comfortably, glad for the fire and the good company. Something happens, though, when you sit around the kitchen during a snowstorm. You *need* to be doing something. A quick check of our impoverished kitchen was a real discouragement. We didn't have the fixings for anything as sinfully fun as fudge, or brownies, or crepes, or even popcorn for that matter. All we could come up with was a head of cauliflower. Cosmic Mike bounced the big head of cauliflower in one hand, and assured me in his best Texan drawl, "Don't you worry, honey, I'll take care of this here little cauliflower for yew." Ever since, I've had Cosmic Cauliflower to remember Mike by when he's gone.

1 head of cauliflower, broken into flowerets
1 cup flour
Equal parts tamari sauce and water
Lots of bacon fat

Add enough tamari and water to the flour to make a nice smooth sauce. It should stream smoothly off the end of a spoon, and the color should be a medium brown.

Heat a cast iron frying pan half full of bacon fat

COSMIC CAULIFLOWER, *continued*

over medium heat. By handfuls, put the cauliflower into the sauce and stir lightly to cover all surfaces. Test the fat with a droplet of water for proper temperature; if there is no sizzle, raise the heat.

Rapidly drop the cauliflower into the fat. Turn the flowerets as they brown. Drain on paper towels. Serve with more tamari sauce.

The point of Cosmic Cauliflower is that the bacon fat cooks the sauce and seals a coating around the flower. When you bite into a piece the coating is thick and crispy and tastes vaguely of bacon; the inside is tender and sweet and steaming. What sets this recipe apart from regular tempura cooking is the bacon fat. Also, there are no eggs in the sauce, so it's a little more basic. Don't be afraid to add an egg if you want to. I have been short of tamari and added an egg. It merely makes the coating a little lighter and tempura-like.

Cosmic cauliflower is sort of like "found objects" in art. It uses almost no ingredients, and it can delight people. That day so long ago in that kitchen so far away now, we bit into our first cosmic cauliflowers, oh so gingerly, not sure what to expect from the mad wooden spoon of a mad philosopher. Our first reaction, as I recall, was that it tasted like fried scallops. That day in the snow, we were transported. Our imaginations ran away with us. We were eating boring old cauliflower, the only thing to eat in the house, and dreaming grand dreams. Never was such a rich meal enjoyed. Cosmic, indeed . . .

15
JANUARY

CHRISTY'S BANANA BREAD

9/20/93
EX

Christy White is a legendary figure in Vermont. She knows everyone and everyone knows her. She's a wonderful woman, but her fame for banana bread has really made her into some sort of legend up in the hills. No matter how many ladies' teas, pot luck suppers, or stuck-in-the-mud parties I've been to over the years, the question is usually posed sooner or later. Maybe I tend to hang around the food table too much, but sooner or later, I hear it: "Hmm . . . banana bread. Hey, Franny, did Christy make this banana bread?" A nod to the affirmative and the asker will take two slices; negative, and he takes a tenuous nibble.

Well, look out world, here it comes. From a scribbled note on the back of a torn-off corner of the Bridgewater, Vermont phone book, Christy's banana bread goes public.

Mash bananas until they are creamy. Slightly beat the eggs with a wire whisk. Add the eggs to the bananas.

Melt butter over low heat. Cool butter slightly. Pour into a bowl with the sugar. Add banana-egg mixture and beat together until smooth.

Sift together whole wheat flour, white flour, salt, and baking soda. Add flour mixture alternately to the banana and butter mixture with hot water. Then add walnuts and bake at 350° for 1 hour and 5 minutes. Cool in pans.

Combine topping ingredients and spoon over banana bread.

3 overripe bananas
2 eggs
½ cup butter
1 cup sugar
1 cup whole wheat flour
1 cup unbleached white flour
1 teaspoon baking soda
½ teaspoon salt
⅓ cup hot water
½ cup walnuts, chopped

Topping
2 tablespoons melted butter
¼ cup light brown sugar
½ cup slivered almonds

FEBRUARY

Late Boat Chowder
★ Landlocked Fish Specialties ★
Linguini with Clam Sauce
★ Fish and Shellfish Calendar ★
Feta Scampi
Cooking Lobster
Tartar Sauce for Seafood
★ Cooking with Mustard ★
Spinach Ricotta Dumplings

LATE BOAT CHOWDER

This recipe dates from my Martha's Vineyard days, when visitors always arrived on the last possible boat of the day and I would have to whip up a quick, island-style supper for them. When you need a good, thick New England–style fish soup in a hurry, this is it.

Sauté the onions in the butter over slow heat until they are tender. Then add diced potatoes and reserved broth, cover tightly, and cook until potatoes are fork tender. If you don't have any clam broth sitting around, use 1 cup Atlantic brand bottled clam juice added to 1 cup of dry vermouth, with a little bit of basil and a little bit of garlic powder mixed in. Again, taste test to your preference.

If your fish is uncooked, put it all in a lightly greased baking pan and bake at 400° for about 15 minutes. If it is already cooked, skip that step. The fish will cook more in the chowder anyway, so don't worry if it's not done entirely. If the fish was fried in batter, you should remove the crust.

When the potatoes are done, flake the fish with a fork or cut it into cubes if it is a dense fish like swordfish. Mix it well into the liquid and put the cover back on. Simmer for at least 15 minutes.

When you are close to serving time, add the milk and cream. Make sure that heat is not too high, so that the chowder will not boil. Heat very slowly over low heat until chowder is uniformly warmed.

Pour into bowls. Use a slotted spoon to get chunks of fish and place the chunks in the bottom of each bowl. Stir the chowder around the chunks. Top each bowl with a dollop of unsalted butter and some freshly ground pepper.

3 tablespoons butter
3 small onions, chopped
5–6 potatoes, cut into chunks
2 cups reserved clam broth
  (or see note)
1 pound fish meat, cooked or
  uncooked
1 cup whole milk
1 pint light cream

LANDLOCKED FISH SPECIALTIES

I spent some time in Nebraska once. Fish there meant frozen filets, but the fish inside the packages could never live up to what I had left behind in Boston. What are landlocked fish lovers to do?

I don't know the answer to that one, but I do know a little bit about "preserved" fish. Herring, anchovies, and canned tuna come from foreign countries, and the politics of their capture may be the subject of debate, but if you've just got to eat fish, they're good enough. You can experiment using different marinades and sauces, and see what kind of exotic recipes you can come up with.

Your first stop should be at a deli counter where you should be able to find herring. There are basically two kinds of herring, pickled in vinegar or pickled in sour cream. The sour cream may not be real and the mixture may contain sorbate, so proceed cautiously; herring in jars is especially suspect. But dinner of herring, sour cream, fresh lemon, and fresh asparagus may make you forget that you're a thousand miles from the sea.

Sardines are pretty pedestrian, but they can be used creatively for hors d'oeuvres, served with rye toast rounds and smeared with a good French crock mustard. Steer clear of sardines that are packed in soybean oil. Keep an eye out for sardines in salted or unsalted brine, with no oil added. Sardines are tiny whole fish. It beats me how they catch the little devils.

Anchovies are something that people either love or loathe. They are very salty; when preparing them, do not add any extra salt. If you sauté them, be sure to use unsalted butter. Anchovies are members of the herring family and no self-respecting Caesar salad would be caught dead without them. But you can go beyond Caesar salad and anchovy pizza. Use anchovies as a garnish for salty, spicy hors d'oeuvres. Add them to an antipasto salad for zest. Top a pesto pasta with anchovies. They look great, and even if some people don't like them, someone in the crowd is sure to love them and will eat all. Anchovies can bring out the personality in a dull crowd; they're the one food that is sure to elicit a reaction.

The best anchovies are those imported from Spain or Portugal. You should buy them packed in salt and olive oil.

Tuna is a fish that we all take pretty much for granted in a brown paper bag or in a casserole with potato chips on top. Well, bring your tuna out of the mundane and make it an exciting part of your meals. Make a nice salad Nicoise for yourself with big chunks of tuna, or add tuna to an antipasto. You can toss tuna flakes with parsley, olive oil, and freshly grated Parmesan cheese for a nice pasta sauce. When it comes time to buy tuna, it's going to be in a can on the shelf in the supermarket. But combined with fresh ingredients from the farmers market, it will be a real treat.

LANDLOCKED FISH SPECIALTIES, *continued*

The six shelves full of tuna can be confusing until you learn to read the tuna labels. The price will pretty much tell the story, but be on the lookout always for good buys on the better cuts of tuna. *Solid* means that the fish in the can has no waste tissue at all; if you can afford it, buy it. *Chunk* means that the meat probably came from the muscle area, making it okay for sandwiches and dips. *Flake* and *grated* should be avoided, since they have less desirable parts packed with the meat in the can, and you are paying for the weight of the waste, not the meat. Also, you will notice that there is light tuna and white tuna. White tuna is Albacore, the true tuna. It costs more, but it tastes better. The light tuna is a similar fish that may not look as dramatic on a plate but is equal in taste and much more economical in price. You decide.

LINGUINI WITH CLAM SAUCE

Those among us who are not totally blissed out by country living and still love a good sneer have discovered that Fran Lebowitz, author of *Metropolitan Life* and *Social Studies* is the reigning cynic of American journalism. Nobody can make a joke at someone else's expense quite like Fran. And if you ever start to wonder why you don't live in the city, just read a couple of Fran's essays. That's as close as you need to get.

One point that Fran makes over and over again is that linguini with clam sauce is mankind's crowning achievement. I have to agree with her. My life changed when I first tasted this wonderful meal, and if you have never ordered it in an Italian restaurant, this is your big chance to make it in the privacy of your own home and find out what all the fuss is about. Don't worry about liking or not liking clams. If you don't like pasta, though, that's another problem. This recipe is foolproof, and I have included canned proportions for times when fresh is not available or when red tide is threatening the coast. Do try it now.

LINGUINI WITH CLAM SAUCE, *continued*

Don't prepare the sauce ahead of time. When you put the salted water for the linguini on to boil, start making the sauce. And don't wait to eat it either. The consistencies are constantly changing and nothing is worse than sitting down to a plate of dried out linguini with clam sauce—unless it is sitting down to a plate of anything else.

Combine and heat butter and olive oil. When heated add minced garlic and a small handful of chopped scallions or fresh sweet onion. Sauté lightly over low heat until the garlic begins to darken. Add bottled clam juice or clam broth from steamers. Simmer until liquid is substantially reduced, about 3 to 4 minutes.

Chop up leftover steamers or minced clams. Add parsley to sauce and cook over moderately high heat for a minute or two.

Meanwhile, boil and drain linguini. Toss with Parmesan cheese and bits of sweet butter. Pour clam sauce on individual portions.

You can add some white wine to leftover sauce to make a second meal. Luckily, the sauce doesn't last long because it tastes so good; it won't keep well or freeze well.

Almost any pasta is good with this sauce, but linguini seems perfectly suited. Make your own or buy homemade. Wheat pasta is the undisputed match for clam sauce. You might try spinach or artichoke flavored noodles, but the effect is a little less spectacular. Spaghetti works fine, too, but try to use the broader noodle sizes.

4 *tablespoons butter*
4 *tablespoons olive oil*
1 *clove garlic, minced*
¼ *cup chopped scallions*
½ *cup bottled clam juice (Atlantic is a good brand and widely available) or 1 cup leftover clam broth from steamers*
1 *can minced clams or leftover steamers*
½ *cup chopped parsley*
1 *pound linguini*
½ *cup Parmesan cheese, freshly grated*

A CALENDAR OF FISH AND SHELLFISH

Your farmers market fish vendor can be a special friend to you. He can keep you posted on what's in season and what's not. He can help suggest alternatives to what your recipe calls for. And he can help you get the most fish for your money. If your fish vendor isn't helping you, find a new one.

The information in this chapter was supplied by Dale Taylor of the Captain's Choice in Ayer, Massachusetts. Dale is everything that a fish vendor should be. Fisherman, chef, and salesman, he knows fish and he knows people. And he's pretty good at matching them up. The information that Dale shares with his customers is the product of years of research, reading, and exposure to the complex world of fish selling. He's down on the docks early in the morning. He sees fishermen, he talks to truck drivers, and he sells only the best. If I could clone him for all of you out there, I would. But there are more like him, I believe; customers have just got to speak up and ask a lot of questions. That's the only way that you'll get what you deserve: the best.

Dale and I sat down one spring day and tried to put together a very basic buying guide to ocean catch. The dates listed are for the Northeast, but we figured it was okay, since so much of the fish comes from there anyway. At the end of our session, we decided that Dale had too much information stored up in his brain—so keep an eye out at your bookstore for a book on fish by him!

Lobster is still the best thing that the ocean ever gave us, and the price will always be too much for most of us to bear. The only hope we have is to study the market and buy when it is less expensive. Most lobsters come from Maine or the Maritime Provinces of Canada. Canadian lobsters are kept in huge pounds, and exported to the U.S. during the slack seasons, early spring and late fall. They are hard-shelled at that time and are a good buy; hard-shelled lobsters are a little more firm and have more meat per pound than the soft-shelled shedders. Our native lobsters shed their shells when the ocean starts to warm up in the spring. Look for smaller lobsters to shed; the larger "selects" do not shed as often as th smaller ones.

Native lobsters are plentiful from May to December. Look for the best prices from mid-September to late October when the tourists are gone, but the lobstermen are still going out. After December, it's back to the Canadians.

Steamer Clams are available all year round. Dale can look at the size and shell pattern of a steamer clam and tell you what bed it came from. I am personally hooked on the Essex clams from the north shore of Massachusetts; they're clean, uniform in size, and very sweet. Be sure to ask your fish vendor where his clams came from, and always keep an ear out for reports of red tide, a bacteria that contaminates shell-

A CALENDAR OF FISH AND SHELLFISH

fish so they cannot be eaten. Clams may be scarce in the winter, during periods of "deep freeze," when the diggers can't get through the ice on the tide flats. The price fluctuates accordingly. Red tide is most common in June, July, and August, so watch for good buys on steamers in the spring and fall. A clambake may sound ideal in August, but one in October might find you on a deserted beach with fresh apple cider and clams that you can afford.

Quahogs belong to a family of mollusk that is cousin to the clam. Their availability follows that of steamers although they are gathered in the shallows instead of in the tide flats. Big bull rakes are used to gather quahogs; the tines of the rake catch the shells. Quahogs fall into three categories. The smallest are *littlenecks*, or *topnecks*. A bushel of them has 300 to 400 littlenecks in it. To determine their size, the shells are dropped through varying-sized rings into different baskets. Cherrystones are slightly bigger than littlenecks; you can find 180 to 250 cherrystones per bushel. Chowders are the big fellows, with only 150 or less in a bushel. They get their name from their ultimate fate: New England clam chowder. A couple of those boys will fill the bottom of your bowl.

Mussels. Does your fish dealer have mussels? If, so, are they cultivated or natural? Find out. Mussels are free for the taking off rocks and wharf pilings in salt water, but you never know for sure what's in harbor water, so ask before you go off on a mussel hunt. They're also a big project to clean. Restaurants and fish dealers usually offer cultivated mussels which are grown underwater where there is plenty of food for the mussels. The cultivated type are clean and tend to have bigger, tastier bodies. The cost can fluctuate—and will, once mussels really catch on. Mussels, by the way, may taste better in the colder months. They are best when harvested from the ocean when the water temperature is 58° or lower.

Shrimp are usually imported—which also means frozen; you may as well accept it. The benefit is that shrimp are available all year round and in different sizes and prices. Ask where the shrimp you buy come from; the best are from Mexico, Peru, and Ecuador.

If you're buying a lot for shrimp cocktail, it might be more economical to pay an extra dollar per pound for bigger ones, and save yourself an hour or more of labor. This is the kind of information that your fish market friend should offer. And if he or she tells you that the origin of the shrimp is unknown, move on. Every box of shrimp is marked with the country of origin. If they don't know, it's because the shrimp were bought in ice chunks from another dealer.

A CALENDAR OF FISH AND SHELLFISH

Scallops are to be had in three kinds: sea scallops, bay scallops, and calico scallops. The largest and most flavorful are the sea scallops, which are also the most expensive, of course. Smaller scallops will be either the *bay* or the *calico* type. Bay scallops are either northern bay scallops (also known as Cape scallops) or southern bay scallops, which are harvested off North Carolina. Calico scallops from Florida are tiny and really cheap; they don't have the taste of a "real" scallop but they'll do in a pinch. To give you an idea of the range of sizes, a pound of scallops will include 10 to 50 sea scallops, 40 to 90 bay scallops, and 90 to 150 calico scallops.

Smaller scallops are available either hand-shucked or steamed open and shucked by machine. Obviously, the steamer will affect the taste of the scallops, but the machines also bring the price down. The decision is yours to make.

Most scallops are available year round, either fresh or frozen. Look for the best prices in the spring.

Squid, or calamari, is an underrated, undereaten delicacy. It is available all year, and it is a great bargain. Look for whitish-gray skin on the squid you buy. The more purple the skin, the more inferior the quality. According to Dale, there is no best time of the year to buy squid. Just follow the harvest; squid is always cheap with a capital C.

Bluefish has a lot of taste and a lovely texture and color. It is one of the more interesting fish and one of the most misunderstood. Some fish vendors would like us to think that there are two varieties, Cape bluefish, which is very expensive, and Boston bluefish, which is only slightly less so. But Boston bluefish is just expensive pollock, so don't fall for that line. Bluefish travels north as the water warms up. In New England, you can get fresh native bluefish starting in July or so, but well before that the fish is available from the Carolinas, Chesapeake Bay, and Long Island Sound. When you can get it fresh, buy it and enjoy it. But it's not a fish that freezes well, perhaps because of the density of the meat and its unique flavor. For best buys, wait until midsummer, then eat bluefish every night for a week. You can cook it a dozen different ways and never get sick of it.

Cod, the sacred fish of Massachusetts, is available all year round. It's most expensive in midwinter, and most economical in midsummer. For best quality, buy in March, April, and May. Don't be fooled if the fish market offers you "scrod." Scrod may have been legitimate fish once, but now it is basically a catch-all phrase for small filets of haddock and cod. Buy it only if it's a good deal.

A CALENDAR OF FISH AND SHELLFISH

Flounder follows cod's schedule, pretty much. It is thin in the spring, and usually the cheapest then, too. The best quality comes in the late fall, although your best bet for quality and price combined is probably to buy it in the summer. When you are considering flounder, ask what type of flounder it is. Winter flounder and blackback are available all year. Summer flounder, also known as fluke, is only available in the summer months. Dabs and yellowtail are around all year. See sole for more information about flounder.

Haddock is a prize fish, fast becoming scarce probably because it is so versatile. Haddock is never cheap, but it doesn't matter. When you need a fish you can depend on, depend on haddock. It is good fresh or frozen, and available all year. The quality is generally consistent, too. Look for your best buys in June.

Hake is a former bargain that has caught on in the restaurant scene in the last few years. It's not cheap anymore, probably because of its popularity. Hake is a deep-water fish that is caught in Georges Basin. The best quality comes from the coldest waters; the meat tends to turn mushy in the warm waters. Hake spoils easily, so be selective when you shop for it. Stock up in the winter and freeze some; it will retain its flavor and texture well in the freezer.

Halibut, or "white swordfish," is always good and always around. Try to get steaks from a fish that weighed 20 pounds or less; steaks from a larger fish may be tough and grainy. If your dealer doesn't know what size fish the steaks came from, the steaks were bought frozen and pre-cut, and aren't fresh.

Ocean Perch, also known as redfish or Norway haddock, is available all year. Oddly enough, ocean perch is the only fish in the western Atlantic that bears its young live. You may recognize the flavor of ocean perch, since it is the main ingredient in those all too familiar fishcakes and fish sticks. Ocean perch is a healthy fish to eat. It is the leanest of the ocean fish and also the lowest in sodium. Its mild flavor is just right for anyone who is squeamish about strong-tasting fish. Just be careful: eat it quickly, for it spoils easily.

Pollock is the social climber of the fish world, often getting passed off at a higher price as the imaginary "Boston bluefish." By that name, you may have eaten it many times. At its real price, you'll enjoy it more. Pollock is available year round, with best buys in late spring and early summer. Dale says to try it with a tomato sauce.

Sea Bass is a real delicacy. It is very expensive and there aren't bargains on this one at any time. It is available from early spring to late fall. If you can't resist buying it, look for small fish (½ to 2 pounds), and steam or bake it.

A CALENDAR OF FISH AND SHELLFISH

Sole is on the menu of every restaurant that needs a token fish dish. So what is it? Sole is really flounder. It is available at the same time and its price fluctuates the same way. Grey sole is witch flounder, and lemon sole comes from large blackback flounder. And Dover sole? Only in Europe will you find such a fish.

Butterfish is the smallest member of the marlin family. It has no real season, but it's cheapest in midsummer. Buy lots of these little guys, because there's not much meat on them. And don't freeze them or any other fatty fish, except salmon.

Mackerel is easy to find from April to October. The best ones are those caught in late summer and early fall. If you can, try some smoked mackerel or smoke your own.

Salmon is the only fatty fish that freezes well. Once you've got it, you can keep it. The problem is getting it.

When it is available, it is likely to be prohibitively expensive, particularly Atlantic salmon. The East coast version is available in the spring, but there is a limited quantity. Each state has different laws, designed to preserve the species but not to provide you with salmon dinners.

Pacific salmon is available in three types. Chum and choho types have pinkish meat, and king salmon has dark red meat. The best buys are in late spring, and the fish is most abundant in early July. The price will vary with availability.

Striped Bass, or "stripers," are not commercial fish but rather sport fish. They're not widely available, but they sure taste good, so get out that rod and reel and head for the surf. If you can find them in a fish market, they'll be expensive. Like the bluefish, stripers move from south to north as the summer progresses, and laws for catching them vary from state to state. An interesting fact about striped bass: stripers are found on the West Coast because they were transplanted there in the late 1800s.

FETA SCAMPI

In a large pan, sauté the onion in butter until golden. Stir in herbs and tomato sauce, and cook over low heat for about 45 minutes.

While the sauce is cooking, wash the shrimp and remove shells. Sauté shrimp and garlic lightly in olive oil. Pour shrimp and garlic into a foil-lined baking pan, and bake for 5 minutes at 400°.

Remove shrimp from oven, and slide back into the skillet. Add lemon juice and wine. Stir and cook for a couple of minutes. Then put back again into the baking dish and pour tomato sauce over all. Reduce oven to 250° and bake for 5 minutes.

Remove scampi from oven and stud with feta cheese chunks. With a wooden spoon, give sauce a whirl to coat, and heat cheese chunks.

Serve immediately with pasta and freshly grated Parmesan.

½ cup finely chopped onion
2 tablespoons butter
1 cup canned tomato sauce
1 teaspoon dried oregano
1 teaspoon dried basil
1 teaspoon dried thyme
Pinch of crushed red pepper
Pinch of salt
Freshly ground pepper
1 pound medium shrimp
2 cloves garlic, chopped
2 tablespoons olive oil
1 tablespoon lemon juice
2 tablespoons red wine
1 cup feta cheese chunks
Parmesan cheese

COOKING LOBSTER

Fill kettle big enough for all the lobsters with water to about two thirds full. Set to boil.

When water is boiling rapidly, drop in the lobsters, head first and place a lid on the pan quickly. When the water begins to boil again, time the lobsters according to weight:

1 pounders = 5 minutes after second boil
1¼ pounders = 6 minutes after second boil
1½ pounders = 7 minutes after second boil

Lift lobsters out of water and allow to cool before serving.

SCALLOPS IN CIDER SAUCE

Remove scallops from refrigerator and allow to come to room temperature (about 30 minutes). Pat scallops dry with paper towels.

In a heavy skillet, melt butter over low heat. Do not let it burn. Sauté the shallots slowly.

When the shallots are soft, add cider to the skillet. When mixture is warm, place the scallops, which have been sliced on the diagonal if they are sea and left whole if they are bay, in the cider. Poach the scallops over medium heat for 2-3 minutes, then remove. Put the scallops on a heated dish.

Slice a Baldwin apple into the remaining liquid mixture and simmer until liquid has been reduced by half. Put the scallops on a bed of wild rice or rice pilaf and pour the mixture over all. Serve immediately with parsley for added color.

2 *pounds scallops*
4 *tablespoons unsalted butter*
3 *shallots, minced*
1 *pint apple cider*
1 *Baldwin apple*
Parsley

TARTAR SAUCE FOR FRIED FISH AND SEAFOOD

Prepare 1 cup homemade mayonnaise. Add parsley, scallions, tarragon, sweet gherkins, and green olives. Season with your favorite mustard, to taste.

1 *cup homemade mayonnaise*
1 *teaspoon parsley*
1 *teaspoon scallions, chopped*
1 *teaspoon dried tarragon*
1 *teaspoon sweet gherkins, chopped*
1 *teaspoon green olives, chopped*
Mustard

COOKING WITH MUSTARD

This cookbook is filled with recipes that call for mustard. In most cases, I have specified either a creamy or grainy mustard; in most cases, it has been Pommery. Pommery is actually a brand name that I use as a common description for any seeded mustard from the Dijon region of France that comes in a crock. When I say creamy mustard, I mean a creamy Dijon—not French's hot dog mustard.

A crock of mustard is the single most used spice in my kitchen. The crock always stands ready to add flavor to the blandest vegetables and meats. If I had to name a single ingredient I could not cook without, it would be mustard.

Experiment with a crock of mustard. It may seem expensive ($5 or more per crock), but the crock will last for months. I smear it on pork chops, chicken breasts, asparagus, blood sausage—anything!

Mustard, so the French legend goes, gets its name from the French phrase *"Moult me tarde,"* the slogan of the Dijon region, meaning "Much awaits me." Much awaits the cook who is creative with the mustards of that region of France.

The one thing to remember about cooking with mustard is to add it to the meal at the end of the cooking time. Do not let it boil, as it will turn bitter. And be careful with amounts. The amounts in these recipes are based on the grainy, seeded Pommery types. If you prefer creamy mustard, you may have to adjust measurements.

Mustard stimulates the appetite, the French say. When mustard is served as a seasoning, there is stimulation aplenty.

SPINACH RICOTTA DUMPLINGS 5·20·87 V.V.G.

Not for guests. Bit messy

Trim and wash about 2 pounds of fresh, leafy spinach (in winter, use 3 to 4 packages of frozen spinach, unbuttered). Cook the spinach for about 2 minutes in boiling water to which you have added salt. Drain off the water and rinse the spinach under cold running water. Press spinach to get remaining water out. Put spinach through food mill or "grate" setting on a blender.

Melt butter in a medium saucepan. Add ricotta cheese, flour, egg yolks, salt, and nutmeg. Stir everything together, then add Parmesan cheese and spinach. Stir until spinach is well mixed in and green color has spread through mixture. Pour into a bowl and refrigerate for 2 to 3 hours.

Remove mixture from refrigerator and decide upon a shape. You can, at this point, roll it out with a rolling pin and cut into shapes or just break off pieces and roll with your hands into small dumpling-like balls. No matter what shape you choose, roll the dough in loose flour and drop into boiling salted water. You may want to use a basket, as you would for deep fat frying, or a long-handled slotted spoon. As the dough balls rise to the top of the boiling water, remove with spoon.

These pastalike creations are delicious with almost any type of meat or on their own as a main course. Choose a light, thin sauce that will not overwhelm the delicate flavor of the spinach. Crumbled bacon in a lemon–white wine–butter sauce is a good accompaniment.

2 pounds spinach, or
3–4 packages frozen spinach
4 tablespoons unsalted butter
2 cups ricotta cheese
2 tablespoons flour
2 egg yolks
Salt
Nutmeg
½ cup freshly grated
    Parmesan cheese

— I used leftover melted butter with lemon + garlic (used for artichokes - to dip)
+ added crumbled bacon & tomato concassé.

MARCH

Spinach & Sunflower Seed Soup
Steamers with Herbs
★ Herbs ★
Moules Mariniere
Baked Haddock
in Sour Cream and Dill
Kielbasa Dinner
New England Boiled Dinner
French Fries Deluxe

The Big Fried Potato Pie
★ Pears ★
Pear Glace
Carrot Cake
Cream Cheese Filling
Cream Cheese Frosting
★ A Special Occasion ★
Glazed Fresh Fruit
for Cake Decorating

SPINACH AND SUNFLOWER SEED SOUP

Heat 2 tablespoons of the butter in a large skillet over medium heat. Wash and cut up the scallions into tiny ¼-inch pieces. When the butter is melted, sauté the scallions gently; when they are tender, remove the pan from the heat.

Open the three cans of chicken broth (or use your own chicken broth if you have some on hand) and pour the contents into a heavy kettle. Turn the burner on medium-high heat. Keep an eye on the broth. Just when it is ready to begin a hard boil, stir in the butter and scallion mixture, the sunflower seeds, and the salt. Bring to a boil and simmer for about 1 hour, or until the kernels are swollen and tender. Turn off the heat and remove pan at this time.

Meanwhile, melt the other 1 tablespoon of butter in the skillet. When it is melted, pour in the white wine and bring to a simmer. Do not let it boil. When it is hot and steaming, add the spinach and sauté it in the mixture until it is wilted and reduced in size. Sprinkle with rosemary and nutmeg.

Allow both pans of ingredients to cool at room temperature for about half an hour. Then drop a spoonful of each into a blender and blend at low speed. Continue to add spoonsful until the blender is full. Empty the blender into a nearby kettle. Continue this process until all the ingredients have been blended together. Then heat the soup gently over low heat until steaming. Serve piping hot with a nut or fruit bread.

3 tablespoons butter
5–6 scallions with tops
2 cups sunflower seeds
     (unsalted)
½ teaspoon salt
3 cans of chicken broth
1 teaspoon dried rosemary
1 pound dried, cleaned and
     trimmed spinach
1 cup of white wine
½ teaspoon nutmeg

STEAMERS WITH HERBS

So you bought all those steamers at the market . . . what now? You can make yourself the most delicious steamed clam feast yet with a few herbs and a little bit of time.

All the clams you've got
1 quart dry vermouth
2 tablespoons garlic powder
2 tablespoons basil
Handful of black peppercorns
2 tablespoons oregano

Take time to look over the steamers, and chuck out any that have badly broken shells. Rinse the clams if you are going to steam them right away. If not, let them sit in their own water.

If you are in doubt about the quality of the clams, you can soak them overnight in sea water and a little bit of cornmeal.

My friend Dale, the fish man here in town, can tell what river bed a clam has come from just by looking at it. I like just about all clams, but I can understand why some people don't like clams at all. Some clams *are* pretty bad. There can be any number of reasons why (sand, mud, bad weather), but a good cleaning, a good checking, and this recipe will save any clam. And with good clams, this recipe will take you out of this world. . .

I should add that I made this recipe for years by carefully following a recipe in *The Martha's Vineyard Cookbook.* My husband loved the recipe, but decided that he wanted to get the same result *his* way without looking at a recipe. So this is a cooking technique, not a recipe. And save every drop of the broth for chowder stock! Note: The measurements in this recipe are very approximate.

Fill the bottom of a large cooking pot (big enough for all your clams) with a mixture that is one-half vermouth and one-half water. You won't need much of either. Just fill the kettle about an inch deep. Add herbs and stir lightly. Then add the clams. (My husband always forgets the herbs and puts the clams in

STEAMERS WITH HERBS, *continued*

first. He then sprinkles the herbs over the clams and it still tastes great.) Steam until the shells open up. Discard any that do not open.

With a slotted spoon, serve up the clams into soup bowls or dinner plates. Strain the broth into a tall pitcher and serve at the table for drinking or for table top clam washing. Serve the customary melted butter with the clams. Aren't they great?

HERBS

If you are really interested in herbs, check out the annual program in Shaker herbs at the Hancock Shaker Village in Hancock, Massachusetts, near the New York border. The Shakers were specialists in herbs and their methods of growing and cooking with herbs are the state of the art.

I personally prefer fresh herbs, but when your rosemary plant shrivels up in December because it was twenty-four degrees in the kitchen when you got up this morning . . . you've got to reach into the cupboard for your backup supply of dried herbs.

There's another reason that I prefer fresh to dried herbs, and that is because of the lack of uniform quality in pre-pared herbs. For years, I bought herbs at health food stores that sold them in bulk, or else I would buy large house-brand containers in supermarkets. In-variably I found the dried herbs to con-tain stems and rough pieces, not just fine, dried blossoms. I got discour-aged. Rosemary, basil, thyme and the other "rough cut" herbs were just a little too rough for my cooking. Some of the more high-priced packages of herbs, like those found in gourmet food stores, were more reliable; I guess you do get what you pay for. But when rosemary is $2.50 for a little thumbnail of a bottle at the gourmet store and you can grow yourself a whole herb garden for the same price . . . which would you rather do?

In general, use the rule of thumb that when a recipe calls for a tablespoon of fresh herbs, you can substitute a tea-spoon of dried herbs. Don't worry about it when you follow my recipes, though. I am very approximate with my measurements, and for a good re-ason: I know that the finished product will be a hit if you follow the basic directions. You probably know by now what proportions of herbs you prefer, and you can adjust my directions to fit your liking anyway. I've transcribed these recipes as I like them to taste. You may not agree with me, but when you come to my house to eat, that's how it will taste.

MOULES MARINIERE

For mussels still in their shells

Debeard and clean each mussel individually under cold water. Scrub thoroughly.

   In a heavy saucepan, large enough to hold all the mussels, or in a small enameled kettle, melt butter. Saute garlic until tender. Pour in dry vermouth or white wine, along with basil, tarragon, thyme, and oregano. Increase heat as you place steamer rack holding mussels inside the pan.

   Steam until all shells are open, discarding any that don't open. Place mussels in 4 shallow soup bowls for serving as an appetizer. Strain liquid from pan and pour over shells, adding more heated wine if necessary. Sprinkle dried parsley and paprika over all. Garnish with baby steamed potatoes and steamed beet slices.

For mussels removed from shells and bought frozen

Prepare liquid as above, but simply sauté mussel bodies for 3 to 5 minutes, until tender. Serve as an appetizer. Pour just enough liquid over mussels in serving dish to keep them moist. Serve bread on the side for mopping up leftover liquid.

3 pounds fresh mussels or
*1 pound frozen mussels
   (removed from the shell)*
4 tablespoons butter
2 cloves garlic
*1 cup dry vermouth or white
   wine*
*1 tablespoon each of the
   following dried herbs:
   basil, tarragon, thyme,
   and oregano*
Dried parsley
Paprika
*Small steamed potatoes and
   beet slices*

BAKED HADDOCK IN SOUR CREAM AND DILL

Haddock's price fluctuates, so I buy a lot when it's inexpensive and freeze it. In September, when there's lots of fresh dill, I pull out frozen haddock and make this dish. I also use this recipe with dried dill weed in other seasons. It's a great "disguise" for fish that is not the freshest; the taste of the sauce is so distinctive it will make a memorable meal.

Wipe the fish dry with paper towels—do not wash it. Lay the fish, skin side down, in a greased, shallow baking pan. Preheat the oven to 350°.

Mix together the sour cream, mayonnaise, celery salt, pepper, thyme, and paprika, and pour it over the fish. Use a spatula to spread sauce evenly. Cover the fish with fresh dill, or sprinkle liberally with dill weed. Bake at 350° for 40 minutes or until fish flakes easily. Serve with parsley garnish and a slice of lemon.

2 pounds fresh or frozen (thawed) haddock
2 cups sour cream
½ cup mayonnaise
1 teaspoon celery salt
½ teaspoon pepper
¼ teaspoon thyme
½ teaspoon paprika
Enough fresh dill to cover or 1 tablespoon dried dill
Sliced lemon
Parsley for garnish

KIELBASA DINNER

Mix together wine and water and pour into the base of a steamer unit or large kettle. Place kielbasa, wrapper removed, in basket of steamer or in bottom of pan. Steam gently over medium-high heat for 15 minutes. Drain and remove to a platter.

Meanwhile, boil or steam potatoes. Add peas at the last minute and steam for 60 seconds or so. Toss vegetables with wine vinegar and olive oil, just enough to coat vegetables. Add vegetables to platter with kielbasa and serve.

1½ pounds Kielbasa
1 cup Beaujolais table wine
½ cup water
4 medium-size round white potatoes
½–1 pound fresh, frozen, or canned peas, in pod or loose
Olive oil
Red wine vinegar

NEW ENGLAND BOILED DINNER

My husband loves this meal. I personally could live without it except for the fact that I could *not* live without the fantastic sandwiches made from the left-over corned beef. Experiment on your own with winter vegetables, picking and choosing the ones you like.

At least four hours before you plan to eat, take the corned beef from your refrigerator and set it in a colander in the sink. Wash it thoroughly with the sink sprayer and then set it in a pot with enough cold water to cover. Let the corned beef sit in this water bath for 20 to 30 minutes. This will help to draw out any excess saltiness. You want the corned beef to be salty, but you don't want it to be inedible.

Drain the water bath off the beef and put the meat in a big kettle. Pour boiling water over the beef, and cook it in simmering water for 90 minutes.

Then add the cabbage, carrots, and turnips. Cover the kettle and let them cook, undisturbed, for an hour or so more.

At the end of the hour, add the onions, parsnips, and potatoes, and cook for half an hour. Test the corned beef by piercing with a sharp fork. If it is tender, it is ready.

Remove corned beef to a cutting board and cut into thick slices. The first cut will tell you if it is done to satisfaction or not; it should be tender and aromatic. Arrange the vegetables on the platter around the beef slices and serve.

To brighten things up, you may want to garnish the platter with hard-boiled eggs and parsley blossoms.

4 *pounds corned beef*
1 *small cabbage, quartered, with outer leaves removed*
3 *carrots, peeled, washed, and cut into sticks*
6 *medium sweet onions, peeled*
6 *small parsnips, washed and peeled*
6 *medium potatoes, washed*
2 *small turnips, peeled and washed*

FRENCH FRIES DELUXE

Wash potatoes and remove any eyes or sprouts. Cut into cubes, slices or french fry sticks. Dip potatoes into flour and then into egg-milk mixture. Fry potatoes in about an inch of oil until brown and crispy. Drain and blot dry.

4 *large potatoes*
Flour
1 *beaten egg*
¼ *cup milk*
Vegetable oil

THE BIG FRIED POTATO PIE

This treat, which is equally good for brunch, lunch, or a late night supper, is a cousin of the much-loved potato pancake. The potato pancake of our dreams is here; it's fatter, more filling, and there's lots of it.

4 *large potatoes*
1 *medium onion*
Blended vegetable oil
Sour cream
1 *teaspoon chives*
1 *teaspoon paprika*

Peel potatoes and soak in cold water until ready to use. When ready, grate the potatoes on a standard grater. Peel and grate onion and add it to the potato.

In a medium-sized skillet, heat blended oil. When the oil is sizzling, pour in potato and onion mixture until the bottom of the pan is covered. Make sure that the potato mixture covers the bottom and fills the sides to a depth of about ½ inch.

Cook over medium heat for about 5 minutes. A spatula inserted under the pie should show the bottom to be turning a golden brown. If it is burning, reduce heat immediately. Increase heat if it seems mushy and sluggish.

When properly golden, gently lift pie out and place it on a platter for a minute. Add more oil to the pan and when it is heated flip the pie back into the pan and cook the other side. Before you flip it back, make a slight hollow about 3 inches in diameter in the second side. Fry until golden.

Lift finished potato pie onto a serving plate, hollowed side up. Fill the hollow with sour cream, to which paprika and chives have been added. Slice into wedges and serve with cold meat.

PEARS

Pears are one of the overlooked delicacies in American kitchens. Americans have not welcomed the pear into creative cooking with open arms, and it's hard to tell why. Since pears are available year round and are one of the easiest fruits with which to work, it just doesn't make sense. Americans love to eat pears as a snack, but how long will it be before they look beyond the fruit bowl and into the complementary tastes of the pear?

There are many ways that pears can be substituted for more exotic seasonal fruits for fresh flavor in the winter months, when strawberries are unheard of and oranges taste like cardboard. Pears are good with meat, baked like apples, or puréed as a sauce base. Experiment and see what you can do with them. You'll be hooked.

Pears are heralded in the fruit market world as the one fruit that can be successfully picked before ripening. Growers claim that they improve with age. The theory is that the starch in the fruit converts to fructose after the pear is picked, and this conversion actually enhances the fruit's flavor. Having grown up with pear trees, I think that one bite into a tree-ripe pear would refute that theory in about ten seconds. But no matter. Fruit growers have been able to supply us with pears all year, and for that we should be grateful. They have also been able to develop more than 500 kinds of pears.

Pears, by the way, are a much bigger deal in Europe than here in the United States, and most of the varieties can be found there, not here. In the U.S., pear growing is centered around the Pacific Northwest and the Northeast. In late summer and fall, the really fresh native pears come rolling into markets from the Northeast, and the Washington–Oregon crop peaks around Christmas. The rest of the year, the pears you find in markets are from Australia and New Zealand, South Africa, and Argentina. Some European pears find their way here in the summer.

Anjou, Bosc, and Bartlett are the three most popular and widely available pears. The Anjou is a lovely shade of green and is an excellent all-around pear. Look for a uniform light green color. Most Bosc pears are from South America. Don't let the dull brown color discourage you if you are looking for pears, and the Bosc is all that is available. It is excellent. The Bartlett is the most common pear, and it, too, is likely to be from South America. The lovely yellow color is its trademark, although it may be speckled with brown.

Regardless of what type of pear you look at, consider cost and quality of fruit over the type. Buy what is available, but only if it is of comparable cost to other seasonal fruits and the fruit is of good quality. Keep an eye out for pears that are on the hard side but that feel spongy near the stem end. You might think that sponginess is a sign of

PEARS, *continued*

the ripening process, but it is more likely to indicate that the pear was picked too early in its growth phase. Your top priority in fruit selection should be either uniform firmness if they are to be stored or used for cooking, or uniform ripeness—"give" in the skin under your thumb, but not breaking through—if you are going to eat all six on the way home in the car (it happens). Blemishes are not a big deal with pears. Don't pass up a good, ripe pear because of a few spots. Better a blemished one than an underripe one.

If you do buy pears for eating or cooking and find them to be cement hard, leave them in a dark place for a few days. Wrap loosely in a cloth or paper bag and check on them frequently. Before you know it, they'll be ready to eat.

I've included some recipes here for using pears, but would like to encourage all you creative cooks out there to experiment with pears and meats. Also, be sure to garnish a cheese board with sliced fresh pears for a real treat.

PEAR GLACÉ

Put the pears in a blender and blend at medium speed until they are puréed. Combine sugar, wine, and water in a pan and stir gently over medium heat. Add pears quickly, before they turn dark. Stir and cook for one minute.

Chill the purée for about 1 hour. Stir in lemon juice, and turn into a mold. Freeze for several hours in the freezer before serving. To loosen from mold, dip outer edge of mold in hot water.

Serve with sprigs of fresh mint and garnish with slices of fresh pear.

4 cups peeled, sliced fresh
  pears
2 cups sugar
2 cups white wine
2 cups water
Juice of one lemon
Mint sprigs

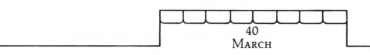

CARROT CAKE

In a large mixing bowl, combine oil and sugar with a wooden spoon. Beat in the eggs, one at a time.

    Sift together flour, cinnamon, baking powder, baking soda, and salt. Add dry ingredients to the oil mixture. Next, fold in the carrots and nuts.

    Pour batter into three 9-inch round cake pans that have been greased and floured. Bake at 350° for 40 minutes.

    Spread cream cheese filling between layers and frost top and sides with cream cheese frosting.

1½ cups oil
2 cups sugar
4 eggs
2 cups flour
2 teaspoons cinnamon
2 teaspoons baking powder
2 teaspoons baking soda
2 teaspoons salt
3 cups grated carrots
1 cup chopped nuts

CREAM CHEESE FILLING FOR LAYER CAKE

Beat cream cheese with vanilla. Add 1½ cups of milk or more, to make a smooth filling. Spread between layers of carrot cake and top with frosting. For variety, add 1 tablespoon of grated orange peel to filling.

8 ounces cream cheese
1 teaspoon vanilla
1½ cups milk

CREAM CHEESE FROSTING

With electric beaters, cream butter and cream cheese until well softened and light yellow in color. Add vanilla extract. Fold in confectioners sugar a little bit at a time and stir with a wooden spoon until desired spreading consistency is reached. Thin with milk if needed.

8 ounces cream cheese
12 tablespoons butter
2 pounds confectioners sugar
2½ teaspoons vanilla extract

A SPECIAL OCCASION

The next time you are called on to provide a spectacular dessert for a special occasion, don't panic. And don't reach for the nearest can of ready-spread sugar frosting either. Head for the market and buy your decorations fresh from the vendors.

Some of the celebratory cakes and desserts that I have built over the years may have overdone it a bit, but I always took the opportunity to experiment. Sometimes I would use the whole cake as a base for a sculpture of berries and fresh flowers. Lots of times, the things that I put on top of a cake were not edible, like the time Alicia and I made a banjo cake for a friend's birthday—with dental floss strings on the banjo. My own wedding cake was a spiraling ramp of marzipan animals and musical instruments, with a 6 inch marzipan unicorn on top leaning against a marzipan gold record. As I said, it's easy to overdo it. But these desserts surely do attract attention.

I recommend that you experiment around as I have done. Buy some tubes of ready-made marzipan at an Italian market and learn how to sculpt with it. Use the berry/fruit glazing technique described in the following recipe to put a glossy touch on fresh decorations. I recommend using blueberries for writing messages on birthday cakes. Cream cheese frosting seems to be "in" right now, so that will always make a crowd pleasing base. Make lots of it.

Remember that you don't have to make a cake for a special occasion. Just as layer, loaf, and bundt cakes lend themselves to different decoration techniques, so do different baked goods. You can also make cookies, pies, and breads with decorated messages. A chocolate pie is a good base for decorating, and with a special loaf of bread, you can incorporate a message into the bread itself with glazing or braiding.

Whatever you do, don't despair. Once I spent a whole day making a "record" cake for a country rock singer and had it presented to him on stage. Either he was blinded by the stage lights or the effect didn't make it. He leaned into the microphone and announced to the concert audience: "Somebody just handed me a cow plop." Back to the drawing board!

GLAZED FRESH FRUIT FOR CAKE DECORATING

Wash all the fruit and drain well. Remove any imperfections with a paring knife. Depend on the apricots and strawberries for the base of your design and begin arranging them all over the side and top of the cake. Use the blueberries to write a message or to fill the spaces between the fruit. The colors will dazzle you.

Boil the jelly in a small saucepan and pour it over the finished fruit design. It will "set" the fruit and give the whole cake a brilliant glaze. You're ready to surprise!

Fresh strawberries

Fresh blueberries

Fresh or canned apricots

1 10-ounce jar of apple jelly

APRIL

★ Avocados ★
Avocado Puree
Roquefort Cheese Dressing
Garlic Mayonnaise
Your Own Peanut Butter
★ Liver ★
Barbecued Chicken Livers
with Apples
Chicken or Duck Livers Bavarian

★ New England Spring Lamb ★
★ Cooking Chart for Lamb ★
Roast Lamb
Lamb Curry
Rice to Serve with Curry
Barbecued Leg of Lamb
Lemon Bread
Streusel-Filled Coffee Cake
★ An Ad That Really Works ★

AVOCADOS

I haven't made a big deal out of avocadoes in this book because I tend to take them for granted. The recent surge in the popularity of what I call "California cooking" has made the avocado a household word. Here in the Northeast, avocados are more plentiful then ever before. Just a few years ago you could not buy them in a chain supermarket. You had to go hunting for a gourmet seller in the marketplace, and then, if you were lucky, you could find a hard-as-rock avocado to ripen on your windowsill. Well, the proliferation of avocado trees in plant windows across the country tells the story: the avocado has arrived.

I prefer to use avocados in a close to natural state, mostly out of paranoia that I might overcook the little devils. They turn bitter if they are overcooked, so watch out. If you must heat a dish with avocado in it, do just that: heat it, don't cook it.

Avocados are great in green salads or sliced and served cold with other vegetables and fruit. You can stuff them with exotic fruit and seafood salads or you can turn them into lovely, delicate sauces, salad dressings, and dips; and none of these requires cooking.

Never expect to serve avocados on the spur of the moment. Avocados control their own destiny, more or less. If you rush to the market on a Saturday morning expecting to find a half-dozen ripe avocados for dinner that night, you will certainly be disappointed, for that day all the avocados in the market will be hard as rocks. Back to the drawing board.

I learned a trick once, long ago, from a chef friend. It may well be an old wives' tale, but you've got to believe, right? I just didn't think before I took a catering job for a couple of dressing-room buffets at a rock concert. Guacamole is always popular with rock stars (the pale green color of the dip may remind them of their pale, unhealthy complexions or something), so I ordered a case of avocados — 48 of them—for delivery the day before the concert. I didn't think. I just didn't think.

The avocados came neatly packed in a premolded container case and they were as hard as rocks. I had asked the wholesaler to send me the ripest he could possibly find. I even told him that appearance didn't matter and they *still* came in the form of small boulders. So I pulled out my friend's solution and gave it a try.

For twenty-four hours, those avocados sat in a vat of white flour. In this case, it took almost ten pounds of flour to cover them. They just sat there until just before I was ready to peel and mash them. And do you know what? It pretty much worked. I had about a half-dozen unusable ones that sat on my windowsill for a few days to ripen naturally, but I used the rest to make the biggest mound of guacamole I ever saw. The musicians gobbled it up, so it couldn't have been too bad; but I don't recommend this as a solution except in desperate situations.

AVOCADOS, *continued*

When you are shopping in the market for avocados, keep your needs in mind. If you want to serve several avocados at once, buy ones that are uniformly ripe. But if you want to have some around to eat for awhile, pick out avocados at varying stages of ripeness.

The only rule for choosing avocados is the old "rule of thumb": press the fruit with your thumb and see what happens. A ripe avocado will give. A half-ripe one will give just in the skin, and an unripe avocado will hurt your thumb.

A problem that you may encounter with avocados is a darkening of the meat, especially if you are filling halves with salad for a colorful meal. Brown avocado meat is not colorful. There is a reason why so many avocado recipes contain lemon juice, and that is because the lemon juice has a chemical property that stops the color change. Sprinkle lemon juice on avocado meat as soon as you peel and cut it.

If you are ripening avocados on a windowsill, stagger the feast by refrigerating them at intervals. When you return from the market, put all the avocados but one or two in the refrigerator. Ripen those on the windowsill. The next day, put out another. If your avocado quota is filled, put half-ripe fruit back in the refrigerator to slow them down. A little bit of thought will go a long way to control the destiny of your fruit and improve the quality and variety of your avocado feasts.

AVOCADO PURÉE

Extra avocados? Never happens. But if it does, you can find many ways to use avocado in a meal, besides for stuffing and salads. A good base is this simple avocado purée. Use it as a base for avocado salad dressing or as a sauce for fish, chicken, or vegetables. Use it quickly and be careful when cooking to only heat—not cook—the avocado meat.

Peeled meat of 1 avocado
2 tablespoons lemon juice
½ teaspoon cumin
2 tablespoons white wine

Mash together all the ingredients with a flat wooden spoon in a flat-bottomed dish until they have a smooth, creamy consistency. Add more wine if necessary to make it smooth. Heat gently over low heat or in a stainless steel mixing bowl inside a water bath, for warm meals; or chill for summer night dinners. For extra tang, add garlic oil droplets or a tablespoon of the liquid from a jar of pickled jalapeno peppers.

ROQUEFORT CHEESE DRESSING

Roquefort isn't Roquefort unless it comes from France. Blue cheese and bleu cheese are made in the United States; no matter how you spell it, it's just not the same. Gorgonzola is a cheese of the same type that comes from Italy.

This dressing recipe is as much a dip as a dressing. It is thick and creamy, and may be served with a salad or raw vegetable plate.

Combine all the ingredients and refrigerate for 1 hour before serving. If you want to use it as a salad dressing and think that this mixture is too thick, cut down on mayonnaise and add more milk.

½ cup mayonnaise
½ cup sour cream
3 tablespoons whole milk
2 tablespoons fresh lemon juice
⅔ cup crumbled Roquefort

GARLIC MAYONNAISE

Put whole eggs and egg yolks in a blender and beat at high speed. Add lemon juice and beat again. With the motor on, pour in enough imported olive oil to thicken the sauce. Turn off motor and add crushed fresh garlic and some fresh parsley. Blend again. If necessary, thin with lemon juice or thicken with more olive oil.

Do not try to substitute garlic powder or commercially prepared garlic for fresh. It just won't taste the same. This sauce is a delicious accompaniment to fresh asparagus. A dollop of Pommery mustard (or your favorite) can expand this sauce to formerly unexplored realms of taste experience.

3 whole eggs
3 egg yolks
3 tablespoons lemon juice
Olive oil
4 cloves garlic, crushed
Handful of parsley, chopped
Pommery mustard

FOOLPROOF HOLLANDAISE

Separate three eggs; reserve whites. Place yolks in blender and beat at high speed. Add lemon juice and beat at high speed again. Add a pinch of salt and pepper and butter, 1 tablespoon at a time, beating at high speed after each addition. When sauce is thick, it's ready. If allowed to sit, it may become too thick. If so, add an ice cube and beat again for just a second.

3 eggs
3 tablespoons lemon juice
Salt and pepper
Melted butter, cooled

YOUR OWN PEANUT BUTTER

Buy 2 cups of unsalted dry-roasted peanuts at a health food store or from a nut vendor. Try to get them shelled; if not, sit down and shell them yourself.

2 cups dry-roasted peanuts
1 tablespoon peanut oil

Put a handful of peanuts into your blender. Add peanut oil to make a liquid base and blend at medium speed for a few seconds. You can keep the top off the blender and watch. When the peanuts are all broken up and are becoming paste-like, turn off the motor. Scrape the butter into a mixing bowl. Repeat until all the peanuts are buttered.

With a wooden spatula, mix the different batches of butter together and transfer to a container for storing in the refrigerator.

LIVER

Liver is not one of my favorite meals, to say the least. But I must admit that after years of fighting it, I have found ways to enjoy liver, and try to buy it often when I can find it fresh.

I confess that I have not experimented with veal liver, which is supposed to approach the sublime in flavor. The big stumbling block has been the price—sometimes more than $3 per pound in the Italian stands.

Most of my experience is with chicken livers, which have to be the ultimate bargain in today's food scene. I buy them from the butcher in the market in five-pound tubs, and separate them in different sized containers for freezing. I put up several small packages for hors d'oeuvres and pasta sauces, and bigger packages for sautéed livers as a meal or for paté.

No matter what your favorite kind of liver is, you can buy it fresh (if you look around) and enjoy a great meal. The same rules apply for all liver recipes: keep the liver cool until you are ready to actually cook it, and don't cook it ahead of serving time. Bring it to the table sizzling hot. And, please, do not overcook liver. Even if you like your red meat well-done, spare the poor liver. Cook it in a hot oven or pan, and leave the inside a cool, moist pink. Don't limit your liver dishes to beef liver and onions or a pork- or chicken-liver paté. Grow up and discover liver on your own!

BARBECUED CHICKEN LIVERS WITH APPLES

Prepare coals at least an hour before you plan to cook. Plan to eat immediately when the chicken livers are done.

Arrange the chicken livers in an alternating pattern with apple slices on long shish kebab skewers. As the livers cook, brush them with a mixture of soy sauce, butter, vinegar, and sugar, using a pastry brush. Turn livers often, allowing 1 to 2 minutes per side, depending on heat of fire. Remove from heat and lay on bed of rice or pasta on serving plates. Grate the Parmesan cheese over all, and serve very hot.

1 pound chicken livers
1 or 2 firm apples, sliced
½ cup soy sauce
¼ cup butter, melted
½ cup tarragon vinegar
1 teaspoon sugar
Freshly grated Parmesan cheese

CHICKEN OR DUCK LIVERS BAVARIAN

Roughly chop chicken or duck livers, leaving them in large pieces. Melt 4 tablespoons butter in a large, heavy castiron skillet. While butter is melting, chop mushrooms and slice onion into half-rings.

Sauté the onion in the butter until the onion becomes soft and yellow. Add livers and increase flame under pan. Stir the livers frequently and shake the pan to loosen them. When all sides of livers are light brown (red of blood is gone), quickly add 2 more tablespoons butter.

Swirl the butter around the pan until it melts. Then add the mushrooms, stirring constantly. (Use a wooden spoon, so as not to break mushrooms.) Sprinkle tarragon over all.

Pour cognac over liver mixture and allow to simmer until liquid is reduced to half its original volume. Remove from heat.

Stir in cream. Return to a slow burner, and allow cream to warm; then serve.

1 pound duck or chicken livers
6 tablespoons unsalted butter
½ cup chopped mushrooms
1 medium-sized onion
1 tablespoon dried tarragon
½ cup cognac
½ cup heavy cream

NEW ZEALAND SPRING LAMB

How can anything that sounds so perfect really *be* so wonderful? With a name like New Zealand spring lamb, there has to be a catch—but there isn't. A chef once told me that the lamb imported from New Zealand and on sale in your supermarket in your little corner of the world may be the finest meat you can buy.

The meat industry in New Zealand is a little more enlightened than the meat industry in the United States. First of all, the meat is totally free of chemical treatment. Yes, it is pure. All sex hormones, tranquilizers, and tenderizers are banned by government law in New Zealand.

Lambs in New Zealand live a carefree, natural life, however short it may be. They are raised, slaughtered, aged, cut, inspected, and flash frozen in New Zealand, and then shipped here. And yes, they are killed in the spring.

When buying lamb, the cut makes all the difference. The most preferable and most expensive cuts are the best, and you may not be able to get them without going to a butcher. Try for the crown roast, the saddle, the rack, and settle for a leg as last resort for a roast. You can buy a leg with the bone in, the most common way that you will find New Zealand lamb in the supermarkets here. A boneless leg of lamb makes a nice meal but, in general, the leg may contain up to 50 percent more fat than a better cut.

Cooking a lamb is generally a matter of taste, but if lamb to you conjures up memories of stringy, gray-brown meat, do yourself a favor with your New Zealand spring lamb. Roast it only until the meat thermometer reads about 135° or so. From your first forkful of pink, tender roast, you will be hooked.

The recipe that follows is excellent for a boneless leg roast. If you have a good cut of lamb, go for the best. Roast it according to the following timetable, serve with wild rice and asparagus tips, and enjoy. Don't worry about gravies or sauces because you won't need them.

ROAST LAMB

Use a large roasting pan, about 4 inches longer than your roast. Sprinkle bottom of pan with olive oil.

In the bottom of the pan, lay carrots, celery, onions, and green pepper. Lay the lamb roast on the vegetable bed and sprinkle liberally with salt, pepper, thyme and rosemary. Rub garlic over roast or sprinkle with garlic powder.

Cook roast at 350° for 15 minutes per pound. Reserve juices for gravy. Place roast on serving platter.

Place roasted vegetables in a blender and purée at high speed. Place saucepan with roasting juices on a burner over medium heat. Add puréed vegetables and more seasonings if desired. Stir until smooth and well-blended. Serve with lamb.

Lamb roast
2 carrots
2 celery stalks
2 onions, quartered
1 green pepper, quartered
Salt and pepper
Thyme
Rosemary
2 garlic cloves

Cooking Chart for Lamb

Cut	Oven	Minutes per Pound	Thermometer When Done
Baby	450°	10 for rare, 12 for pink	150°
Roast Leg	325°	12–15 for pink	135°
Crown	325°	12–15 for pink	135°
Lion	325°	12–15 for pink	135°
Rack	375°	12–15 for pink	135°
Saddle	325°	12 for pink	145°
Boneless	325°	10 for pink	135°

ESTELLE AND MORTON SOSLAND'S LAMB CURRY

This curry recipe won a cooking contest.

Heat oil in a stew pot. Add garlic and onion, and sauté together for a few minutes. Add bay leaf, cinnamon, and cloves. Stir to mix, cover and cook on low heat for 5 minutes.

Add lamb to the pot. When the water has steamed off the meat, add salt, pepper, cumin, coriander, paprika and curry powder. These last additions should be carefully stirred into the meat to avoid burning. Cover ingredients with water and add tomatoes. Cover and cook slowly until meat is tender.

Serve with cooked rice (recipe follows) and condiments.

½ cup oil
4 garlic cloves, chopped
3 large onions, chopped
1 bay leaf, crushed
1 teaspoon cinnamon
6 whole cloves
3 pounds lean lamb, cubed
1½ tablespoons salt
1 teaspoon black pepper
1 teaspoon cumin
1 teaspoon coriander
1 tablespoon paprika
2 tablespoons hot curry powder
2 tomatoes, skinned and chopped

Condiments

Minced crystalized ginger
Chutney
Hard-boiled eggs, minced
Crumbed cooked bacon
Shredded coconut
Parsley, chopped finely
Chopped peanuts
Grated orange rind
Currants

RICE TO SERVE WITH CURRY

Sauté two onions in vegetable oil. Add as much rice as you want to cook and sauté rice until slightly brown. Cover with chicken broth, place in a casserole dish, and bake at 350° for 45 to 60 minutes. Check rice occasionally and add more chicken broth if needed.

BARBECUED LEG OF LAMB

Track down a butcher at a large market in the city and get the butcher to help you pick out a suitable leg of lamb for barbecuing. It helps if they can "butterfly" the leg for you so it will lie flat on the grill or coals.

Marinate the lamb in the ingredients listed for at least 8 hours. Prepare the coals at least an hour before cooking. Wrap freshly peeled potatoes, carrots, and whole peeled small onions in an aluminum foil envelope, and lay them in the coals.

Lay the lamb leg directly on the grill and let the juices drip down into the fire (watch out for rising flames). Use a turkey basting bulb to put more liquid on the meat as it cooks. Open the vegetable envelope; add a few drops of marinade. Roll the vegetables in the juice and move them to a hotter spot on the grill to brown before serving. Check lamb with a meat thermometer (should read about 140°) or slice open and check for the right color. *Do not overcook.* Serve sizzling hot with the vegetables.

Half a leg of lamb, butterflied

Marinade

1 *cup dry vermouth*
3 *cloves garlic*
2 *lemons*
2 *Handful of peppercorns*
½ *cup olive oil*
⅓ *cup tarragon vinegar*

Potatoes
Carrots
Baby onions

LEMON BREAD

Cream shortening and 1 cup sugar together. Add eggs and beat in. Sift together flour, baking powder, and salt. Add flour alternately with milk. Pour into an 8-inch bread pan that has been greased and floured, and bake for 45 minutes.

As soon as the bread is removed from the oven, mix together lemon juice and ½ cup sugar. Spoon it over the bread until all is absorbed.

I found this recipe at the Vermont Farm Show in Barre in 1974. The recipe and I have been together ever since, and I have enjoyed making and eating this bread many times. It is an excellent dinner bread, but can really brighten up a cup of coffee in the morning, too.

½ cup butter or margarine
1½ cups granulated sugar
2 eggs
½ cup milk
1½ cups flour
1 teaspoon baking powder
½ teaspoon salt
Juice of one-half lemon

STREUSEL-FILLED COFFEE CAKE

Heat oven to 375°. Grease and flour a 9-inch square pan. Mix thoroughly sugar, shortening, and egg. Stir in milk. Sift dry ingredients together, and stir into wet mixture.

Combine streusel ingredients. Spread half the batter in pan. Sprinkle with half the streusel mixture. Add remaining batter and sprinkle remaining streusel on top. Bake for 30 minutes.

Cake ingredients

¾ cup sugar
1 egg
1½ cups flour
½ teaspoon salt
¼ cup butter or margarine, softened
½ cup milk
2 teaspoons baking powder

Streusel ingredients

½ cup light brown sugar (packed)
2 teaspoons cinnamon
½ cup chopped nuts
2 tablespoons flour
2 tablespoons melted butter

AN ADVERTISEMENT THAT REALLY WORKS

Your farmers market can get the attention of the community you are trying to sell to with any number of advertising ploys. One that will work without fail, though, is a team or hitch of draft horses.

Draft horses are back, and chances are that you will be able to find someone in your area with a team. If you can't think of anyone, consult a local or regional draft horse owners association or a breed association. These groups exist to promote their horses, and they will find someone to help you.

There are many ways that draft horses can publicize your market. The hitch of horses can become the symbol of your market, and pull a fresh vegetable float in a parade. They can march through town on a Saturday morning announcing the opening of the farmers market. They can stand quietly in the parking lot, munching hay and bringing traffic to a halt. Everyone will want to stop and say hello to a team of draft horses.

Another way to involve draft horses in your publicity efforts is to take your show on the road, so to speak. Load up a flatbed wagon and have the horses draw the load through town, selling as they go. The driver can have a prescribed route from parking lot to field to town green where people can stop by and pick up some produce. Or, you can serve a special need by sending the team to the local housing unit for the elderly and having the residents purchase their produce off the wagon. You can do the same thing with a truck, of course, but the draft horses will create an indelible image in people's minds. Elderly people especially will enjoy the horses and reminisce about the era of the horse, and you will have done a real service.

MAY

★ An Indoor Herb Garden ★
★ Gardening Chart for Herbs ★
Stuffed Grape Leaves
Tandoori Chicken
Asparagus Sunrise
Asparagus Vinaigrette
★ Decorating Your Stall ★
Creamed Asparagus Soup
Red Snapper with Green Sauce
★ Fiddleheads ★

Fiddleheads with Lemon Butter
Fiddlehead Potato Salad
Stir-Fried Fiddleheads
with Scallops and Carrots
Fiddleheads in Horseradish
Dandelion Green Salad
★ Mint ★
Mint Julep
Strawberry Rhubarb Cobbler
Strawberry Rhubarb Custard Pie

AN INDOOR GARDEN OF HERBS

Wouldn't it be nice to be able to pick fresh basil leaves in the middle of winter to flavor a sauce? With a little bit of planning, you can enjoy the pleasures of fresh herbs year round. The place to start is your farmers market.

Start your indoor herb garden in the spring if you can. At the farmers market, try to find small "starting" pots of different herbs. When you get home, transplant the herbs to traditional clay pots or to a large wooden planter. What herbs you can't buy as starter plants, sow as seeds either in planters or in the earth.

The trick to successful indoor gardening is what you do with the plants outdoors. If you have clay pots, you can dig holes in the ground and submerge the pots. The earth will keep the herb roots cool, and when fall comes you just have to lift the pots out of the ground and carry them into the house. If you use a large wooden planter keep a careful eye on the moisture content within, and water whenever the soil gets dry, which might mean every day. Keep up with the soil's needs by supplying a water-soluble fertilizer once a week.

If it's not spring, and you've got the urge to start some herbs, go right ahead. Basil, oregano, chives, and parsley plants are available year round in greenhouses and even in some grocery stores. Transplant them as soon as you get home, and keep a close watch on the plants to insure a healthy start. For convenience, find a sunny kitchen window to house your herb collection. You can keep a close eye on them there and snip off fresh herbs as you need them.

When it comes to planting, try to plant herbs of similar heights together in planter boxes: parsley, rosemary, chives, tarragon, and chervil are good starters for a planter. Or you might use a hand turned ceramic "strawberry" planter—a hanging or standing pot with little ruptures in its sides in which you can plant different seedlings or seeds. Plant the tall herbs, like rosemary, dill, marjoram on the top, where it is open and there is plenty of room for growth. In the side pockets, plant smaller herbs or even a scented geranium.

You will notice immediately that an indoor herb garden adds a few lively new smells to your cooking area. The odors will hopefully remind you to use the herbs, and to experiment a little. You'll never know what you might come up with—and you've got everything to gain.

GARDENING CHART FOR INDOOR HERB GARDEN

Parsley	Biennial	6–12″	Available in flat or curly leaf types
Dill	Annual	3–4′	Hard to grow indoors
Oregano	Perennial	2–2½′	Start from seeds or a cutting
Basil	Annual	1–2′	Harvest leaves only
Marjoram	Perennial	1–2′	Harvest leaves only
Thyme	Perennial	2–12″	Harvest leaves only
Rosemary	Perennial	2′	Cut back regularly to control growth
Chervil	Annual	1–2′	Harvest leaves and stems
Chives	Perennial	1–2′	Start from plant, not seed
Tarragon	Perennial	1–2′	Start from plant, not seed
Bay	Perennial	3–6′	Plant in a tub; dry the leaves
Mint	Perennial	2–3′	Try different varieties
Savory	Annual	12–18″	Keep it pinched back to control growth
Sage	Perennial	20–30″	Encourage bushy growth with trimming

STUFFED GRAPE LEAVES (DOLMADES)

You often find stuffed grape leaves in their chilled state as an appetizer at a party, but I also like to eat them hot as part of a dinner. I find that they are excellent with lamb and chicken dishes, and can spice up a bland meal. Serve them hot or cold, depending on the weather. I usually cook them in the late spring, when I can pick grape leaves that are young and still tender. If you do not have a grapevine handy, you may have to buy bottled grape leaves packed in brine. Be sure to rinse them well before you add anything to them.

Sauté the onions in olive oil, stirring constantly. When they are lightly golden, add 1 cup of boiling water, rice, and nuts. Cover the pan and let the rice cook. Do not peek for about 15 minutes. Then lift a corner of the lid and check to see how much liquid remains. If liquid is gone, remove from heat. If

1 cup chopped onion
⅔ cup olive oil
1 cup uncooked long grain rice
¼ cup ground nuts
1 can Italian tomatoes
Black peppercorns
Parsley
2 teaspoons dried crushed mint
2 cups white wine
2 tablespoons lemon juice

STUFFED GRAPE LEAVES, *continued*

rice is still standing in liquid, replace cover and cook 5 minutes longer, then check again.

As soon as you remove rice mixture from heat, add tomatoes with juice, and 5 black peppercorns. Sprinkle chopped parsley over all and mix well.

If your leaves are fresh, wash them well with water. Check with vine owner to see if they were sprayed with an insecticide or herbicide. If they were, don't eat them. Buy the bottled kind. If you know that the leaves have been living a good, clean life, proceed.

Let the leaves stand in a colander as you work. Lay them out one at a time on a cutting board. Lay a teaspoon of filling on each one and fold in the sides. Nip off the stem and roll the grape leaf into a little envelope. Then place each one, seam side down, in an oiled baking dish with a flat bottom. Continue filling and rolling until you are exhausted or all the leaves are filled, whichever comes first. You can make as many layers as you want in the dish.

Mix together the wine and lemon juice and the mint. Stir and pour over the grape leaves.

Cover and bake for 20 minutes at 350°. Check occasionally to make sure that the liquid has not all been absorbed. Lift grape leaves out of the dish with a slotted spoon and lay carefully on a serving platter. Serve hot or chilled.

This is a basic recipe. Consult a Greek chef for some serving ideas. If you are going to serve them hot, you might want to consider a yogurt sauce with black olives and peppercorns, or maybe a feta filling for the grape leaves. The ideas are endless and the flavor will always be fantastic. Use this flavor combination as a base, and go on from there.

TANDOORI CHICKEN

Tandoori is an Indian method of cooking; but this recipe comes from Margaret Hanni, my mentor in the kitchen of the Bridgewater Tavern (rest in peace), where it was the specialty of the house. If you decide to cook this meal, cook it right, and eat it while it is still hot and succulent; you will get a little taste of what it was like to sit down to a meal cooked by Margaret Hanni in the world's most casual restaurant. Wish you had been there, but this is as close as I can get you.

Marinate the chicken breasts in the yogurt, to which all the spices and juices have been added and thoroughly mixed. Let the breasts sit in the yogurt mixture for several hours.

When ready to cook and serve, roll the breasts first in the sesame seeds and then the cornmeal. Meanwhile, heat the butter.

Sauté the breasts until they have a golden crust and the meat is cooked inside. To test, pierce with a very sharp knife and check meat color and consistency. Use first breast as a model.

4 boned, skinned chicken breasts split
1 cup plain yogurt
1 teaspoon garlic, put through a garlic press
Pinch of dry ginger
Pinch of chili power
1 cup clarified butter
½ teaspoon sweet or hot paprika
½ teaspoon coriandor or ½ teaspoon cumin
2 tablespoons lemon juice
2 tablespoons lime juice
Sesame seeds
Cornmeal

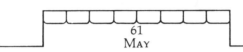

ASPARAGUS SUNRISE

When native asparagus comes into season, take advantage of it, no matter where you live. Here in the Northeast, it comes in around May or so, depending on the severity of winter. My husband and I have a secret patch of asparagus that is overflowing with spears. We eat so much that we almost get sick of it. I never get tired of finding new ways to cook asparagus though. And I also never cease to find fault with rubbery, out-of-season asparagus. Wait until fresh asparagus is available. Then go wild.

Cut and clean asparagus spears; each spear should be about 5 inches long. Steam the spears lightly in equal parts of water and white wine. Drain the spears and reserve the liquid.

In a skillet, heat butter over medium heat. Stir in enough white flour to make a paste. Slowly add light cream to make a sauce, stirring constantly. If the sauce is too thick, add some of the reserved liquid. Simmer the sauce for 5 minutes or until thoroughly smooth and heated.

Cut up a loaf of French or Italian bread. Place thin slices of Jarlsberg or Swiss cheese on each slice and pass under a broiler, with the rack set several inches below the heating element. Let the cheese melt, but do not brown.

Arrange the asparagus spears on the bread. Pour the white sauce over the asparagus. Top with a slice of hard-boiled egg. Decorate with a surrounding circle of paprika.

Asparagus spears (4 per serving)
White wine
2 tablespoons unsalted butter
White flour
½ pint light cream
French or Italian bread
Jarlsberg or Swiss cheese
Hard-boiled egg
Paprika

ASPARAGUS WITH VINAIGRETTE SAUCE FOR ONE

Wash and clean the asparagus. If you prefer, peel the bottom of the stalks. Lay the spears on their sides in a bunch and trim the ends so that the spears are about the same length. Tie into a bunch with kitchen string. Place the asparagus upright in a tall saucepan or kettle. Pour boiling water into the pan carefully, making sure that the spears stay upright. Water should cover asparagus. Boil for 15 minutes.

Pull the asparagus out of the pan and transfer to a low, long serving dish. Mix together the other ingredients in a mixing cup and pour over the asparagus. Then sit right down and eat your treat!

1 *pound asparagus*
Salt, pepper
1 *teaspoon sugar*
½ *cup lemon juice*
5 *tablespoons olive oil*
2 *tablespoons white wine*

DECORATING YOUR STALL AND INCREASING YOUR SALES

Attractively displayed fruits and vegetables are the secret to sure sales. Polish those apples and pile them to the sky, and just wait for someone to come along. Sometimes a stall does need a special touch, and root crops and dried produce may be the answer.

In Europe, garlic and onions are sold in braids. The stalks are left on during the drying process so that the air can circulate through drying vegetables hung high in the rafters. By braiding shallots, garlic, onions, and carrots, you can create attractive displays that will draw every eye to your stall. The display units will sell, too, once customers see how attractive your stall is, and can visualize how great those onions would look hanging in their own kitchens. And to think that they used to buy onions in plastic bags . . .

Carrots can be sold with the tops left on as attractive, colorful bunches. If the tops are long and strong, braid them like the onions. For special color, combine different root crops and sell them at special rates. They will sell quickly!

One of the most attractive and appealing displays that I have seen in farmers markets was a braided wreath of dried red chili peppers. It is unique, attractive, and useful, since you can break off the dried peppers as they are needed. A wreath like this can add a Southwestern touch to a kitchen. Does that give you ideas for Christmas gifts?

CREAMED ASPARAGUS SOUP

You can use leftover asparagus for this soup, if you have some. If you are planning to prepare another recipe that calls for the use of more elegant asparagus tips, just use the stalks for this recipe. No one will ever know, and I won't tell.

Sauté the onion in the butter over medium heat in a heavy saucepan. Add the white wine and the potatoes, and simmer in the wine and butter until tender to the touch of a fork. At this point (probably about 15 minutes or more) add the asparagus, which has been cut up into inch or so slices. Cook for about 5 minutes over medium heat, bringing the soup just barely to a boil. Then remove from heat and run the soup through the blender.

Return soup to the saucepan and add the light cream. Stir it all through the soup and reheat. Add more cream or more wine to get the consistency right for your taste.

Just before serving, squeeze a few drops of lemon juice into each bowl. Top with a slice of lemon and serve hot.

Note: This can also be served cold as a hot weather soup. Just chill individual bowls in the refrigerator without the lemon juice. Add lemon juice at serving time, top soup with a dollop of rich sour cream, and garnish with fresh parsley or watercress and that slice of lemon.

½ *stick unsalted butter*
⅓ *cup chopped onion*
2 *medium potatoes, cubed*
1 *pound asparagus cooked or uncooked*
1 *pint light cream*
2 *cups white wine*
Lemon juice
Lemon slices

RED SNAPPER WITH GREEN SAUCE

Wipe dry the snapper—two filets should be sufficient for four people. Place the fish in a shallow baking dish and preheat the oven to 350°.

Clean and peel potatoes, and set them aside.

Boil fresh or frozen peas for 3 minutes. In the same water, you can then boil one pound of asparagus spears, tied in bundles. Rinse both vegetables under cold water when boiling time is complete and then set aside.

Arrange the potatoes around the snapper in the baking dish. Sprinkle all with salt and pepper. Place the asparagus spears in a criss-cross design over the snapper, taking care that the red color of the fish shows through.

Add sour cream or yogurt to the peas, along with dried parsley. Pour this mixture over the fish, potatoes and asparagus. Sprinkle paprika over all.

Bake in the oven about ½ hour, or until fish is done. Serve in the baking dish. Garnish with parsley flowers if desired.

2 *pounds red snapper*
8 *small white potatoes*
1 *pound fresh or frozen peas*
1 *pound asparagus*
Salt and pepper
1 *pint sour cream* or *yogurt*
¼ *cup dried parsley*
Paprika
Parsley flowers

FIDDLEHEADS

Why am I writing this now? I should be out looking for fiddleheads.

Fiddleheads are the tiny shoots of the ostrich fern, a plant that grows along riverbanks and creek beds, especially in the northern states. If you check religiously every day during the early spring, you will one day find that the ferns are shooting up out of the ground in little, tightly furled heads. The heads are about the size of a silver dollar, although they are perfectly good if they are as small as a quarter. Just make sure that you have the right kind of fern—the wrong kind tastes awful, as I've learned from bitter experience.

Fiddleheads are spiraled tightly like the tuning end of a fiddle, with tiny wisps of brown paper-like sheaths stuck inside the spiral. Before cooking, that sheath has to be removed.

If you are going out to pick fiddleheads, you've got to be there the right day. A day late is literally a day too late. Don't even bother to pick the fiddleheads once they begin to unfurl and stems are formed. They emerge from the ground in the spiral, and you should pick them as soon as the whole spiral is above ground.

On a spring day in Vermont, you can see the rivers patrolled by anxious fiddlehead pickers. Everyone has his favorite fiddlehead patch staked out, so you may have some competition if you plan to pick your own.

Not all the fiddlehead pickers on the shores of Vermont's rivers and streams are fiddlehead gourmets. Many are entrepreneurs who know that the little heads are in great demand on spring dinner tables in Boston and New York and points beyond. And fiddleheads bring a high price, so the hunt is a profitable one.

No matter how you get your fiddleheads, you've got to get them to your kitchen and start to prepare them for cooking. And the process is the same, no matter the source. The State of Maine canning company in Maine sells canned fiddleheads that will do in a pinch if you want some fiddleheads to use as a garnish, but for main course eating, opt for fresh from the market or from your riverbed.

Start with a good, thorough washing. On second thought, make that three or four washings. Fiddleheads are coming out of damp, acidic soil, and they need to be well cleaned. Chances are that your fiddleheads will also still be draped in their brown tendril wrappings, and frequent washes will loosen the brown stuff and make cleaning easier.

When you are satisfied that all the dirt is gone and that no more riverbank floats in the wash water, drain the fiddleheads in a colander and then dump them into a mixing bowl. Take along another bowl for your cleaned heads, and a sharp knife and a paper towel to catch the trimmings. Move to a comfortable chair and begin the tedious task of cleaning. (Fiddleheads are second only to mussels in their need for

FIDDLEHEADS, *continued*

tedious cleaning.) Sometimes a good rub with your thumb across the spiral will loosen the brown matter, but sometimes you may have to insert the point of a knife to loosen the stubborn stuff. Remember that there are two sides to every fiddlehead and clean both of them.

Because of the length of time it takes to clean fiddleheads, you may want to buy just a few for your first meal and then work your way up to a major fiddlehead project. Once the fiddleheads are washed and cleaned, give them a quick run through with cold water to refresh them, and proceed with your favorite recipe or store them in the refrigerator in a plastic bag until you are ready to cook them.

I am giving some fiddlehead recipes here, but I would like to say that almost any asparagus recipe will taste great with fiddleheads substituted for asparagus, and vice versa. The ultimate is a dinner of fiddleheads and wild asparagus. These two spring vegetables are very versatile, the spirit of spring itself. Don't miss them if you can help it.

STEAMED FIDDLEHEADS WITH LEMON BUTTER

Steam the fiddleheads for about 5 minutes or until they are tender enough for you to pierce with a fork. Drain immediately and refresh under cold water. Drain again and transfer to a serving platter.

Meanwhile, melt the butter over low heat, taking care that it does not brown. When melted, remove from heat and add the lemon juice.

Stud the platter of fiddleheads with the lemon slices and pour the butter sauce over all. Grate pepper over the fiddleheads and serve immediately.

You can substitute garlic butter, hollandaise, or your favorite oriental sauce for the lemon butter so that the fiddleheads may complement any type of meal. With just the lemon butter, they make a meal in themselves.

1 quart cleaned and washed
fiddleheads
Steaming water
1 stick unsalted butter
Juice of ½ lemon
½ lemon, cut in thin slices
Freshly ground black pepper

FIDDLEHEAD AND POTATO SALAD

Combine the salad ingredients and put on the bed of red lettuce in a flat-bottomed bowl or serving platter. Combine the dressing ingredients. Chill the salad in the refrigerator until just serving time. At that time, pour 2 tablespoons of the dressing over the salad. Serve remaining dressing in a dish on the table.

1 quart fiddleheads, steamed and chilled
3 large potatoes, boiled and cut into 2-inch cubes
1 medium red onion, cut into rings
Bed of red lettuce
1 cup of snow pea pods, steamed and chilled
2 red Delicious apples, cut into slices

Dressing

6 tablespoons olive oil
1 tablespoon red wine vinegar
1 tablespoon Pommery mustard
1 teaspoon minced garlic
½ teaspoon paprika
2 tablespoons lemon juice
5 black peppercorns

STIR-FRIED FIDDLEHEADS WITH SCALLOPS AND CARROTS

Melt butter with olive oil in a wok or large, heavy skillet. Add the scallops when the oil is sizzling hot. Stir them vigorously for about 2 minutes. Then drop in the fiddleheads and carrots, and stir for about 3 minutes.

Have soy sauce and sherry and sugar mixed together in a small measuring cup at the side of the stove. When vegetables have been cooked to your taste, pour in the sauce and stir again for about 30 seconds. Instantly remove from heat and serve.

1 pint fiddleheads, cleaned and washed
½ pound sea scallops, rinsed and patted dry
3–4 carrots, washed, peeled and cut into sticks
1 tablespoon butter
2 tablespoons olive oil
2 tablespoons dark soy sauce
2 tablespoons dry sherry
1 teaspoon sugar

FIDDLEHEADS IN HORSERADISH

Sometimes fiddleheads can get out of hand. When you've had all your favorite fiddlehead salads and sauces, and there's still a pile on the sideboard, what are you going to do with them? Well, here's a little dish that might make your nose run a little—but it will be delicious. The basic recipe is the same as the ziti with horseradish that my friend Vinny makes when he wants to torture me. This version is a little milder and has a surprising taste to it.

Chop the fiddleheads fine and then sauté over medium heat in the oil. Remove them with a slotted spoon and mix with the ricotta cheese.

Spoon ½ cup of tomato sauce into a deep casserole dish. Top it with a sprinkle of horseradish and a layer of the ricotta and the fiddleheads. Top that with a sprinkle of mozzarella. Repeat layers until you reach the top of the pan or run out of ingredients. Top with tomato sauce and remaining mozzarella. Bake at 350° for 45 minutes. When you remove the casserole from the oven, cover the top with slices of hard-boiled eggs and Parmesan cheese. Let cool for 20 minutes before serving.

2 tablespoons olive oil
2 cups cleaned, rinsed fiddleheads
1 cup grated fresh horseradish
1 cup ricotta cheese
1 cup grated mozzarella cheese
2 cups Italian tomato sauce
Freshly grated Parmesan
4 hard-boiled eggs, sliced

DANDELION GREEN SALAD

Wash dandelion greens under cold running water. Let soak for a few minutes, drain, and wash again. Pick off roots and any brown spots you may find.

Quarter two medium-sized potatoes and boil until a fork pierces them easily. Remove from water, reserving the liquid, and cool under running water. Set aside.

Add wine vinegar to steaming potato water. Place greens in steamer rack and put inside pan. Steam until greens turn limp, but remove before they turn dark green. Refresh under cold running water.

Cook 1 small beet in rapidly boiling water. Drain and allow to cool. When cool, dice beet and potato.

Fry bacon in a cast iron skillet. Drain bacon slices on paper towels and save bacon fat. When cooled slightly, crumble bacon and set aside.

In a glass dish, arrange greens, beets, and potatoes. Pour 2 tablespoons of bacon fat over all and toss gently.

Melt butter in a small pan. Add white wine and heat gently. When warm and steaming slightly, remove from heat. Pour over salad and garnish with lemon wedges. Delicious served hot or cold.

1 bunch dandelion greens
2 medium-sized potatoes
1 tablespoon white wine
   vinegar
1 small beet
4 slices bacon
1 tablespoon unsalted butter
½ cup white wine
Lemon wedges

MINT

You can try to cordon off a corner of the herb garden for mint, but it won't work. Within a year the mint will have spread like wildfire, and it will be everywhere that you don't want it. Rather than fight it, conquer it from the start; plant it in pots or window box containers. Use it as a hedge in these containers on a patio or deck and watch it grow. When it's time for a mint julep or iced tea, you can just lean over and pick a sprig of mint. But don't leave it to its own devices. It has conquest in mind.

MINT JULEP

Chill tall glasses in the freezer for 30 minutes before mixing drinks.

Dissolve sugar lump in water. Using a mortar and pestle, crush mint leaves with the sugar until it is a speckled paste.

Crack ice with a mallet and fill all the glasses with crushed bits of ice to the rim. Stick a sprig of mint in each glass, pour in paste, add bourbon, and serve with a stirrer.

1 lump sugar
1 tablespoon water
4 mint leaves, dried
2 ounces Kentucky bourbon
1 sprig fresh mint

STRAWBERRY RHUBARB COBBLER

Mix together 1 cup sugar with the cornstarch. Stir in cup of water. Bring mixture to a boil and simmer for one minute.

Add strawberries and rhubarb. Pour mixture into greased baking pan and dot with butter.

Mix together 2 tablespoons of butter, biscuit mix, 3 tablespoons of sugar and the cream. Drop spoonfuls of dough mixture onto the hot fruit. Bake at 400° for 25 minutes.

1 cup plus 3 tablespoons sugar
1 tablespoon cornstarch
1 cup water
2 cups strawberries, hulls removed
2 cups rhubarb, cut into 1-inch pieces
Butter
3 cups biscuit mix
1 cup light cream

STRAWBERRY RHUBARB CUSTARD PIE

Beat eggs slightly; then add 2⅔ teaspoons milk and beat again.

Mix together sugar, flour, and nutmeg. Stir this mixture into the eggs. Mix in the rhubarb and gently fold in the strawberries.

Spread 1 tablespoon of softened butter over the bottom of the unbaked pie shell. Pour the filling into the shell, and lay strips of dough in a lattice pattern on top of the pie.

Brush the lattice with any remaining liquid in the bottom of the bowl to which 1 teaspoon of milk has been added. Bake for 50 to 60 minutes at 400°. When cool, brush the top with 1½ tablespoons of confectioners sugar. When the sugar has been absorbed, brush again with 1 tablespoon sugar. Chill pie until ready to serve.

3 large eggs
3⅔ teaspoons milk
1½ cups sugar
4 tablespoons white flour
¾ teaspoons nutmeg
3 cups rhubarb, cut into ⅓-inch slices
1 cup strawberries, sliced
Pie crust
Confectioners sugar

JUNE

Beet Salad
Vinaigrette Dressing
Blue Cheese Potato Salad
Stir-Fried Broccoli & Mushrooms
Ginger Melon Strips
Gingerbread Shrimp
Shrimp & Broccoli in Sesame

Ginger and Soy Steak Marinade
Peng Peng Chicken
Bluefish with Savory Relish
Bluefish with Capers
★ Specialty Display Vegetables ★
Craig's Favorite Cheesecake

BEET SALAD

Boil and peel beets. When cool, slice horizontally and put aside.

Prepare a bed of greens on a flat platter or on individual glass salad plates. Just before serving, arrange the beet slices on the bed of greens and garnish with pitted black olives. Pour vinaigrette dressing over all. Sprinkle with chopped walnuts and diced hard-boiled egg.

2 *large beets*
Greens (spinach, chicory, or romaine lettuce)
Black olives
Hard-boiled egg
Chopped walnuts

VINAIGRETTE DRESSING

In a measuring cup, combine ingredients in order listed.

1 *tablespoon Pommery mustard*
2 *tablespoons lemon juice*
4 *tablespoons olive oil*
Pinch of dried basil

BLUE CHEESE POTATO SALAD

Peel and boil potatoes. While they are cooking, put celery in a blender with onion, salt and pepper, parsley, and enough olive oil to make it blend quickly.

In a large bowl, combine sour cream, blue cheese and enough tarragon vinegar to make the mixture sauce-like.

When potatoes are easily pierced by a fork but not mushy, remove them from boiling water and refresh immediately under cold water. Cube potatoes and add contents of blender and blue cheese sauce. Chill for several hours before serving. Garnish with alfalfa sprouts, radishes, and avocado. Serve on red lettuce or red cabbage decorated with lemon wedges.

4 *large potatoes*
½ *cup chopped celery*
½ *cup chopped onion*
Salt and pepper
3 *tablespoons dried parsley*
Olive oil
1 *pint sour cream*
½ *cup crumbled blue cheese*
Tarragon vinegar
Alfalfa sprouts
Radishes
Avocado
Red lettuce or cabbage
Lemon wedges

STIR-FRIED BROCCOLI AND MUSHROOMS

When you want to eat fresh vegetables quickly, try this shortcut to great flavor and texture.

Heat the oil and butter in a large cast iron skillet or wok. When it is sizzling hot, add the vegetables. Stir the vegetables constantly with a wooden spoon for about 3 minutes. Don't let the vegetables burn. If the oil starts to smoke, remove from heat, but continue to stir.

Just before serving time, mix together the soy sauce, sherry, and sugar. Remove vegetable pan from heat and pour sauce over all. Stir well. Return to heat for a minute or two until the sauce starts to bubble. Serve at once.

2 *tablespoons blended oil*
2 *tablespoons butter*
1 *cup broccoli flowers and diced stalks*
1 *cup sliced mushrooms*
2 *tablespoons soy sauce*
2 *tablespoons sherry*
1 *teaspoon sugar*

GINGER MELON STRIPS

Use a couple of different kinds of melon if you can. This might be a good recipe to use as an excuse to seek out split or damaged melons at the market. I've made this recipe with honeydew, cantaloupe, and watermelon. Watermelon didn't work as well as the more solid melons, but you can experiment all you like.

Remove all the seeds and pulp from the melons and cut them into narrow strips or scoop out balls if you prefer. Carefully pare away the melon rind. Mix together the sugar, ginger, and coconut in a flat-bottomed bowl. Add melon and toss gently with two wooden spoons until coated with the mixture. Cover the bowl and chill strips until serving time. Remove excess sugar mixture. Eat as is or add to a juicy fruit salad.

2 *melons*
Confectioners' sugar, about ⅓ cup
1 *teaspoon ground ginger*
2 *teaspoons grated coconut*

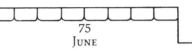
GINGERBREAD SHRIMP

Cook the garlic in the oil and butter in a large, level skillet or wok until the garlic starts to sizzle but do not let it burn. Remove the pieces of garlic with a slotted spoon.

Rinse shrimp and pat dry. Sprinkle them lightly with white wine (just a few drops in the bottom of a bowl), and then dump the bread crumbs on the shrimp and toss lightly. Lift each shrimp and brush off any extra crumbs; you want just a light covering, and the whole shrimp does not have to be coated. Add the shrimp to the butter and oil and sauté until they turn light pink. Stir them gently, making sure that all sides get cooked. When each shrimp is coated with specks of golden, flaky crust, remove from skillet with slotted spoon and allow to drain on paper towels or a clean white cloth.

Stir snow peas and mushroom slices into remaining oil. Toss for a few seconds. Then add ginger root and lemon juice and toss once vigorously.

Lay shrimp on top of spinach bed. Spoon snow peas and mushrooms on top of and around the shrimp. Then pour pan juices over all, adding more melted butter if needed to cover everything.

1 *clove garlic*
2 *tablespoons blended oil*
2 *tablespoons unsalted butter*
1 *pound medium shrimp,*
    peeled and deveined
½ *cup bread crumbs*
1 *cup snow peas*
4 *large mushrooms sliced*
    thinly
3 *tablespoons lemon juice*
1 *tablespoon grated ginger*
    root
Raw spinach for garnish

SHRIMP AND BROCCOLI IN SESAME SAUCE

Sauté the garlic in a little bit of cooking oil. While it is cooking, mix the arrowroot with 1 cup of water. Add 2 cups of water to the garlic and bring to a boil. When boiling, add the arrowroot mixture. Then add the soy sauce and sesame seeds. Cook, stirring, for 5 minutes, or until liquid is reduced by half.

Lay hot shrimp and broccoli flowers on a bed of wild rice, and pour sauce over all.

1 tablespoon chopped garlic
Vegetable oil
⅓ cup arrowroot
3 cups water
3 cups dark soy sauce
1 cup sesame seeds
Steamed broccoli flowers, cut cut up
1 pound cooked shrimp
Cooked wild rice

GINGER AND SOY SAUCE MARINADE FOR STEAKS

Prepare steaks at least one day ahead of planned meal.

Mince and blend equal parts of ginger root and garlic, allowing one large garlic clove per ½ pound of meat. If fresh ginger root is not available, use ¼ teaspoon ground ginger per garlic clove.

Rub the mixture into the meat, piercing with a sharp fork as you go along. Next, sprinkle meat with the soy sauce. Allow meat to sit in juices until you are ready to cook.

Ginger root
Garlic cloves
Japanese-style soy sauce

PENG PENG CHICKEN

The source of this recipe, I know not. It was given to me in the great oral tradition of most recipes—flung over the shoulder of a great cook in mid-magic. In this case, the cook was Margaret Hanni, a wonderful friend who raised my food consciousness a hundred-fold. When she introduced Peng Peng Chicken to the Bridgewater Tavern in Bridgewater, Vermont . . . well, they are still talking about ping pong chicken back there on the shores of the Ottauquechee.

This dish is the perfect combination of exotic and easy. You're going to love it.

Cook chicken breasts in boiling water until done. Shred chicken meat and discard the bones. Reserve the broth for another time; I usually freeze it.

Prepare a low, flat platter with the bed of lettuce and cabbage. The cabbage is a nice touch, but any colorful combination of greens will do. Arrange the greens so they drape over the side of the platter, and arrange the chicken pieces, pepper, and mushrooms on the bed. Cover and refrigerate until serving time.

Mix the remaining ingredients together in a small bowl. Taste often and add more of anything you like. I like a strong garlic-sesame taste, so this recipe is slanted that way. It really makes chicken taste like nothing else.

You can make the dressing ahead of time but don't add the dressing to the salad until 10 seconds before you serve it. This stuff is *potent* and it can overpower you if it sits around and has a chance to penetrate the vegetables.

Spoon the dressing over the vegetables and chicken at serving time and serve cold with a bottle of white wine.

4 *chicken breasts, skin removed*
8 *tablespoons sesame tahini*
2 *teaspoons salt*
8 *teaspoons sugar*
8 *tablespoons soy sauce*
4 *tablespoons white wine vinegar*
8 *garlic cloves, chopped*
8 *teaspoons diced scallions*
½ *pound sliced mushrooms*
1 *green pepper, cut up*
Bed of romaine lettuce and shredded red cabbage

BLUEFISH WITH SAVORY RELISH

The time to buy Cape bluefish is June, when the bluefish tournaments are on. It's also the best time to visit the Vineyard—before the crowds. I make a blue-fish pilgrimage once a year in June to Menemsha to buy a load of the best fresh bluefish from Captain Poole's market there.

Don't let all the spices in this recipe put you off. Bluefish has a stout flavor; it can stand up to exotic spices and condiments and still have a heavenly taste. But if you buy bluefish out of season or aren't sure of the quality or freshness of your fish, this recipe can be very handy to hide an unpleasantly strong flavored fish from the palates of a party of inlaws or business associates. This dish has saved the day for me. One Friday I skipped home from Haymarket Square with my bargain bluefish under my arm (I had had to settle for Boston blue) and when I unwrapped it, I noticed that the meat was not the freshest I had ever cooked. It was still very edible, but this flavorful sauce dispelled my fears. A good recipe to have on hand.

4 pounds split and boned bluefish
¼ cup butter, melted and cooled slightly
2 egg yolks
1 tablespoon chopped onion
2 tablespoons pickle relish
2 tablespoons chopped marinated mushrooms
2 tablespoons lemon or lime juice
2 tablespoons red wine vinegar
Salt and pepper to taste
2 tablespoons Pommery mustard

Preheat oven to 400°. Lay the bluefish in an oiled baking pan big enough for the fish to lie flat. Put the fish in the preheated oven and bake it for 30 minutes. Then pull it out of the oven.

Mix the rest of the ingredients together. Spread the mixture over the fish. Return the fish to the oven and cook another 30 minutes or until the fish flakes when tested with a fork.

Serve this fish with boiled white potatoes, beets, and a simple salad. Let the fish speak for itself.

BLUEFISH WITH CAPERS

Remove bluefish from refrigerator and let it sit at room temperature for one hour before cooking. Unwrap and pat dry with paper towel.

Dribble melted butter around a narrow baking pan. Place bluefish, skin side down, on buttered surface. Sprinkle fish liberally with basil and capers, about half a bottle for 4 servings. Grind black pepper over all and drip 1 tablespoon of caper "juice" on each filet.

Place fish in the middle of a 400° preheated oven. Bake for 20 minutes, testing for flaking. Spoon juices over filets and serve.

1–2 pounds bluefish filets
2 tablespoons melted butter
Dried basil
1 bottle of capers
Pepper

SPECIALTY DISPLAY VEGETABLES

You may be able to pre-package some washed and cut-up vegetables, and increase sales of some less attractive vegetables like beets and turnips and cauliflower at the same time. Invest in a supply of attractively shaped jars of various sizes. Blanch each vegetable for a few minutes in a steamer, and then arrange them in colorful layers in the jars. Pour boiled oil and vinegar over the vegetables, and top the jars with a square of brightly colored cloth or a screw-on top. Mark on the bottle that the contents should be eaten soon and refrigerated immediately. Be sure to use carrots to their full advantage in this project. Add corn kernels for a bright yellow touch.

CRAIG'S FAVORITE CHEESECAKE

To make the crust, crush the crackers with a rolling pin between two layers of waxed paper. Put into a bowl, add melted butter, and toss until the crumbs get moist and lumpy. Transfer the crumbs by tablespoonfuls into an 8 inch spring form pan with 2- to 3-inch sides. Press the crumbs all over the bottom of the pan and up the sides. Prick the bottom of the crumbs with a fork. Bake for five minutes in a 350° oven. Remove from oven, and let crust cool to room temperature.

Begin the filling by creaming the cream cheese with the blunt end of a set of electric beaters. Add eggs and 1 cup sugar, and beat on low speed. When well beaten, add the vanilla. Pour this mixture into the crust and bake for 30 minutes at 350°. At the end of 30 minutes, turn off the oven and let the cake sit in the warm oven for 30 more minutes.

For the top layer, add 2 tablespoons of sugar to the sour cream and then add the almond extract. Pour this onto the top of the cake and bake at 350° for about 5 minutes. Then remove the cake from the oven and put it away for a day or so. When you are getting ready to serve it, lay the strawberries rounded side up on top of the cake, and sprinkle almonds and cinnamon sugar over the strawberries. At this point, release sides of pan and call Craig to come over and help you eat it.

Crust

1 package cinnamon graham crackers
1 stick of melted butter

Filling

16 ounces cream cheese
2 eggs
1 cup sugar
1 tablespoon vanilla extract

Top layer

1 pint sour cream
2 tablespoons sugar
1 tablespoon almond extract
1 tablespoon sugar mixed with 1 teaspoon cinnamon
Halved fresh strawberries
½ cup slivered almonds

JULY

Artichoke Soup
Chilled Broccoli Salad
with Mushroom Slices
Marinated Vegetable Salad
Summer Squash with Fresh Basil
New Potatoes with Dill
Italian Roast New Potatoes
Caviar Mousse

Lemon-Mint Vinegar
Italian Artichoke Hearts
★ Making Selling Easier ★
Zucchini Bread
Caramel-Nut Pound Cake
Watermelon Eyecatcher
Porch Swing Lemonade
★ Apricots ★

ARTICHOKE SOUP

Place artichokes in a large enough pot so they only form 1 layer. Cover with the rest of the ingredients. Bring to a boil, and cook over moderate heat for 45 minutes or until artichokes are done. If it seems that too much liquid is evaporating while cooking, add a little water to the pot.

When the bottoms of the artichokes "give" under light pressure, they are done. Remove bay leaf and as many peppercorns as you can easily retrieve. Serve artichokes with broth in soup bowls. Use soup for dipping and for eating.

6 artichokes, tops and stems trimmed off
1 large can Italian tomatoes
3 cans beef broth, plus three cans water
12 or more black peppercorns
1 bay leaf
Dash of olive oil

CHILLED BROCCOLI SALAD WITH MUSHROOM SLICES

Wash and trim one head of broccoli. Remove leaves if you prefer and shorten stems to about 5 inches. Discard woody stumps of stems. Place the broccoli in a large steamer or kettle with a small amount of water. Steam the broccoli until bright green and slightly tender to the touch of a fork.

Drain broccoli and remove it to a large mixing bowl. Let the broccoli cool at room temperature. When cool, place broccoli in bowl in refrigerator until thoroughly chilled.

While the broccoli is chilling, slice mushrooms (caps should be closed at stem and "gills" should not show) very thinly. Set aside. In a small bowl, mix together olive oil, wine vinegar and lemon juice.

When broccoli is cooled, remove it from the mixing bowl and dice. Return to bowl and add dressing and mushrooms and toss gently. Store in refrigerator until ready to eat. This salad may be used as a decorative accent to platters.

1 large head of broccoli
⅓ cup olive oil
½ cup red wine vinegar
Juice of ½ lemon
½ pound mushrooms sliced thin

MARINATED VEGETABLE SALAD

Cut up and mix together an assortment of the following fresh, uncooked vegetables: mushrooms, broccoli, onion wedges, cauliflower, zucchini, snow peas, green beans, asparagus, artichoke hearts, carrot sticks, cherry tomatoes or tomato wedges, spinach leaves, and the like. Arrange them on a serving platter or place them in a large mixing bowl.

Cut up lemons and squeeze the juice over the vegetables. Then toss the exhausted bodies in with the vegetables for extra flavor. (Remember to remove lemons before serving.)

Make a marinade of equal parts of red wine vinegar and olive oil. Add garlic cloves, paprika, sweet basil, and dry mustard. Mix dressing ingredients together and pour over vegetables. Place a plate over the salad or cover with plastic wrap and let rest for at least 90 minutes before serving.

Mushrooms
Broccoli
Onion wedges
Cauliflower
Zucchini
Carrots
Snow peas
Green beans
Asparagus
Artichoke hearts
Cherry tomatoes or *tomato wedges*
Spinach leaves
Lemons
Wine vinegar
Olive oil
2 *garlic cloves, crushed*
1 *teaspoon paprika*
1 *teaspoon dried sweet basil*
1 *teaspoon dry mustard*

SUMMER SQUASH WITH FRESH BASIL

Remove ends and stem from squash, slice, and steam briefly. Melt butter in a skillet and add squash. Sprinkle lightly with salt, and add fresh basil leaves. Toss in skillet until basil adheres nicely to squash. Turn off heat and add sour cream. Grind black pepper over skillet and serve.

2–4 *small yellow summer squash*
2 *tablespoons butter, melted*
1 *teaspoon salt*
½ *cup fresh basil leaves*
½ *cup sour cream*
Pepper

NEW POTATOES WITH DILL

Quarter potatoes and boil in salted water until done. Drain.

Prepare a mixture of melted butter, vinegar, and chopped fresh dill flowers.

Pour sauce over potatoes and toss gently. Serve with salt and pepper.

4 fist-sized new potatoes
4 tablespoons butter, melted
2 tablespoons cider vinegar
½ cup chopped dill flowers
Salt and pepper

ROAST NEW POTATOES, ITALIAN STYLE

Preheat oven to 350°.

Scrub and peel potatoes, and pat them dry with paper towels or a clean towel. Place potatoes in a shallow roasting pan, with or without other vegetables or meat. Sprinkle the potatoes very lightly with salt and freshly ground black pepper.

Mix together the olive oil, garlic, and parsley in a small measuring cup. Dribble the oil mixture over the potatoes in the pan. Turn the potatoes and continue to drip olive oil until each potato is thoroughly coated and somewhat shiny. Add more of the olive oil mixture if needed. Baste potatoes with oil drippings from pan bottom. Roast potatoes in oven for about 1½ hours, basting frequently with oil drippings from pan bottom. When done, potatoes will be golden colored and slightly crusted on the outside. Serve potatoes on a platter with other vegetables or surrounding a roast.

If you're in a hurry try to find small potatoes, about 3 inches in diameter, and cook for less time. Small potatoes often sell for big prices; watch for them off on their own at produce stands.

6 new white potatoes
2 tablespoons olive oil
1 clove crushed garlic
1 tablespoon dried parsley
Salt, pepper

CAVIAR MOUSSE

In a small bowl, sprinkle gelatin over ¼ cup of cold water. Allow to soften for 10 minutes.

In another bowl, combine eggs, mayonnaise, and Worcestershire sauce. Carefully fold in the caviar.

Put gelatin (still in bowl) in a pan of simmering water, and stir gelatin until completely dissolved. Let cool to room temperature.

Add gelatin to caviar mixture along with lemon juice, and salt and pepper to taste. Combine gingerly.

Spoon mousse into a lightly oiled 1½ cup ring mold, and chill for 4 hours or until set. To serve, dip mold in hot water for a few seconds, and invert onto a serving platter. Decorate center of mold with parsley and lemon wedges, and serve with toast points.

1 tablespoon gelatin
3 hard-boiled eggs, put through a small sieve
½ cup mayonnaise
1 tablespoon grated onion
1 teaspoon Worcestershire sauce
4 ounces caviar
2 teaspoons lemon juice
Salt
White pepper
Toast points
Parsley
Lemon wedges

LEMON–MINT VINEGAR

A bottle of this vinegar makes a nice gift: a few drops turn boiled potatoes into heavenly treats.

Combine all the ingredients in a large mixing bowl. Funnel everything into a quart bottle and close tightly. Turn vinegar upside down once every day for the first week. It's ready to use after a week. This vinegar will not keep indefinitely unless you want to boil the bottles and seal them as if you were making preserves.

1 quart cider vinegar
1 cup fresh mint leaves
3 tablespoons grated lemon rind

ITALIAN ARTICHOKE HEARTS

You will have a hard time collecting a dozen artichoke hearts from an eating binge, because no one will want to give up their hearts. Best to start with canned artichokes. They may seem expensive, but they're worth it. Unless the hearts are in a jar where you can see the size, it's best to buy two cans. If they are very large, cut each in half. If they are small, leave them whole.

Rinse the artichoke hearts under cool running tap water. Drain and prepare other ingredients.

Mix together bread crumbs, flour, and Parmesan cheese. Stir lightly with a fork to distribute ingredients for a light, powdery mixture. In a small bowl, beat the eggs until just mixed, not frothy. Heat ½ inch of oil in the skillet set on medium heat. Keep an eye on the oil and the skillet.

Dip each artichoke heart into the beaten eggs and then dip into the flour mixture. Shake off any loose crumbs and lay the hearts gently into the olive oil. As crust forms, turn the cooking hearts until all sides are golden brown.

Remove the hearts from the oil as they are finished, and drain the hearts on several layers of paper towels or on very clean cotton cloths. When the last hearts are done, pour off the oil into a container to cool. Shake salt lightly over the hearts.

Meanwhile, return the skillet to heat. Melt the butter in the skillet, but do not allow it to brown. Watch the heat closely to control temperature. When butter is golden and bubbling lightly, add lemon juice and stir with a wooden spoon. Return the artichokes to the skillet and sauté lightly, constantly turning them. Transfer to a basket or lined dish,

2 cans of artichoke hearts or twelve freshly cooked hearts
Olive oil
⅓ cup flour
¼ cup Italian-style bread crumbs
¼ cup fresh grated Parmesan cheese
2 eggs, beaten
½ stick unsalted butter
1 tablespoon fresh lemon juice
Lemon wedges for garnish

ITALIAN ARTICHOKE HEARTS, *continued*

cover with a clean cloth, and keep warm in a 250° oven until ready to serve.

Serve the hearts with fresh lemon wedges and the tiny tender inner leaves of a head of romaine lettuce wedged between the hearts. You may wish to sprinkle them with dried parsley for color.

Some people like an oriental sauce or light soy sauce with these hearts, but they are really just as good unanointed. You be the judge.

HOW YOU CAN MAKE SELLING EASIER

If you have an overabundance of one crop or if you had a chance to wholesale an item but weren't able to sell the produce in its natural state, consider selling prepared foods. (Do check health code regulations first, though.) Your buyers may find the prepared version more attractive than the natural state, and if you can afford the labor time that will go into the effort, you will probably be successful. For instance:

Are strawberries going by? Hull and wash the berries before leaving home. Pack a portable stove and the ingredients you will need to make jelly or jam. Make the jam right at your stall. The aroma alone will draw people, as will the offer of a taste test on a piece of freshly baked bread. Sell the jam by the pound in glass jars. Be sure to let people know that the jam is fresh, not preserved, and that it should be eaten quickly.

Rhubarb sales are slow? Follow the procedure for strawberries and make rhubarb sauce or, better yet, combine rhubarb and strawberries, and sell filling for strawberry-rhubarb pie. Who could resist? Try this with raspberry syrup, too.

What about vegetables? You could sell scalloped potatoes, ready to bake, or pureed parsnips, or cut-up vegetables ready for stir-frying in a wok.

What about damaged vegetables? Most people will appreciate a price break on damaged vegetables and fruits that are packaged and cut. A bruised pineapple that is cut into serving-size chunks will save someone time, as will cut cauliflower blossoms.

ZUCCHINI BREAD

In a large mixing bowl, combine eggs, sour cream, sugar, oil, zucchini, salt, cinnamon, and vanilla. Set aside.

Sift together flour, baking powder, and baking soda. Stir wet ingredients once, and add dry ingredients to them, mixing well. Pour batter into 2 greased and floured 8-inch loaf pans and bake at 350° for one hour.

2 eggs, lightly beaten
¼ cup sour cream
1¼ cups sugar
1 cup oil
2 cups grated zucchini
1 teaspoon salt
3 teaspoons cinnamon
2½ teaspoons vanilla
2¼ cups flour
1 teaspoon baking powder
1 teaspoon baking soda

CARAMEL-NUT POUND CAKE

This recipe came from the archives of the Bridgewater Tavern recipe files. No one is given credit for the recipe, but the card is adorned with words of praise and exclamation points (and many flour fingerprints and globs of dried cake batter, the sign of a good recipe) left by subsequent chefs. It's a good one—especially good because of the pecans.

Cream butter and margarine until fluffy. Add the white and brown sugars, 1 cup at a time, and cream thoroughly. Add eggs one at a time, beating after each one. Sift flour, salt, and baking powder together. Add flour mixture to creamed mixture alternately with the milk to which the water has been added. Then add the vanilla and the pecans.

Pour the mixture into a greased and floured 10-inch tube pan. A bundt pan is best. Bake at 325° for 1½ hours.

This cake seems to improve with a day or two of rest. Keep it under a tight-fitting cake holder for best results.

1 cup butter
½ cup margarine
1 box light brown sugar
½ teaspoon salt
1 small can evaporated milk
⅓ cup water
1 cup white sugar
5 eggs
3 cups sifted flour
½ teaspoon baking powder
1 tablespoon vanilla
1 cup chopped pecans

WATERMELON EYECATCHER

2 pints raspberry sherbet
1 pint pineapple sherbet
2 pints lime sherbet
1 cup semisweet chocolate
   chips

Use a round-bottomed bowl as an ice cream mold. Let each pint of sherbet sit out for half an hour before you start to make this dish. It will soften and be easier to work with.

Give each sherbet a good stir with a wooden spoon to loosen up the frozen parts. Then plaster the outer layer of the mold with lime sherbet. Make sure that you cover the whole inner surface, so that no part of the bowl shows.

Inside the lime, spread a thin layer of pineapple sherbet. This will represent the pulpy part of the melon rind, which is rather thin. Make sure that you get a complete covering with the pineapple sherbet. Depending on the size of the bowl you are using as a mold, you may need more of any of the flavors listed.

Empty the raspberry sherbet into a separate mixing bowl. Pour in the chocolate chips, and mix well. Then stuff the whole center of the bowl with the chocolate chip–raspberry mixture. Fill right to the top of the bowl.

Freeze the mold for several hours before serving. To loosen, dip the bowl quickly into a pot of boiling water. Turn the sherbet out onto a serving platter so that it sits on its side. Slice as you would a watermelon and serve.

PORCH SWING LEMONADE

Lemons "on special" hard to resist? The man behind the sign will only sell them in dozen units? Go ahead and buy them and make yourself a stock of lemonade. Don't dismiss this recipe as too obvious—have you ever steamed fresh vegetables in white wine and lemonade (50/50) or added fresh lemonade to a summer soup? It will never go to waste, as long as there are hot, lazy summer afternoons. And with today's labor-free juicers, making lemonade should be a snap.

1 dozen lemons
1½ cups white sugar
Cold water

Soften the juices in the lemons by rolling them under the palm of your hand on top of a good stiff cutting board. Cut one lemon into thin slices. Pick out the seeds and discard them. Cut the other eleven lemons in half across the middle and squeeze the juice out of each one. Go through the juice with a fork and pick out any seeds that have come through the juicer.

In a large bowl, mix lemon juice with the sugar. Add 3 quarts of water and stir well. Give the lemonade the taste test at this point. If you will be serving it with ice, leave it on the strong side. But add more lemon, sugar, or water as your taste dictates.

Transfer the lemonade through a funnel into a gallon storage container and chill until ready to use. If you don't drink it all at first . . .

APRICOTS

I discovered apricots as a political force during my exposure to a tyrannical food coop. The food coop met in the restaurant where I worked as I was preparing for the evening's business. The members of the coop were quite egalitarian, as I recall. Majority did not rule in this coop. Unanimity was required.

At the time, as I am sure it is now, there was a discussion between high-priced Egyptian dried apricots and lower-priced but possibly sprayed California apricots. For weeks, I listened to what I now recall as the Apricot Wars. And for the life of me, I can't recall who won, the Californians or the Egyptians. I do recall lobbyists who arrived early for meetings to try to sway undecided coop members. And I recall impassioned speeches for the Egyptians ("What's money? Your body's at stake here!") and boldfaced accusations ("Well, maybe you can afford it, but I'd rather save the money . . .").

I had never realized how important apricots were to people, although I also think that I may have discovered an isolated pocket of apricot addicts. I set out from that time to investigate the little critters and find out what makes them so special. To this day, when I encounter an apricot, I always inquire as to its place of origin. No purveyor or server has responded with more than a shrug. It was an unpublicized war, I guess.

Apricots, in case you've never been told, originally came to the Western World via the pockets of Marco Polo. The hilly country outside of Peking is the natural home of the fruit, and the Chinese have been enjoying apricots presumably since the beginning of time. California and the Southwest are the only areas in the United States suitable for apricot cultivation, and they are not a lucrative crop. Only about 30 percent of the crop is salable, since the little softees are so perishable. (No wonder they're so expensive.)

You can find fresh apricots in markets only in June and July. Watch out if you buy them at any other time. They are very good dried, and you'd be amazed at all the creative things that you can do with them. Nothing can beat them for a snack while hiking.

AUGUST

First Cucumbers
Dad's Crock of Pickles
Cucumber Salad
Fried Tomato Slices
Tomatoes with Basil
and Sour Cream
Dilled Baby Corn
Corn Grilled in Husks

★ Involving Your Community ★
Fried Pumpkin Blossoms
Zucchini Mikonos
Skewered Swordfish
Mjeddrah
★ Melons ★
Carrot Sherbet
Wild Blackberry Pie

FIRST CUCUMBERS

Simply slice cucumbers and let soak in cider vinegar for about 15 minutes before serving. Grate fresh black pepper generously over all and serve.

DAD'S CROCK OF PICKLES

Summer just wouldn't be summer for me without pickles from my dad's crock. When I decided to do this cookbook, I hounded him for the recipe, which he denied existed. Maybe there is no recipe; it may instead be a ritual. No matter what it is, it's great. These pickles are somewhere between half-sours and deli kosher dills. There's no garlic in them—I guess that's the difference in taste. The fun part is taste testing them. Every day, there are subtle changes in flavor, guaranteed to delight. Some like them saltier than others, but I'll take them just about any old way—and lots of them, please, Dad.

    Wash out the crock and cover the bottom of it with a mass of dill stalks and flowers. Prepare the pickling cucumbers by looking them over carefully. Wash them well and scrub each one with a vegetable brush. Fill the crock to about the ¾ mark with cucumbers. On top of the cucumbers, lay another layer of dill flowers and stalks.

    To prepare the brine, mix hot water (a few gallons) with a handful of pickling salt. Add a handful of pickling spice, and pour it into the crock. Fill almost to the top. Discard any extra hot water. Make sure that all the pickles are covered. Put a large plate on top of the dill, and put a big rock on top of the plate to press everything down. Make sure that no pickles float up around the edges. Leave the crock alone in a dark, cool

1 5-gallon ceramic crock
Lots (at least an armful) of fresh dill flowers and stalks
Pickling salt to taste
Handful of pickling spice
Enough pickling cucumbers (3–6 inches) to fill crock

DAD'S CROCK OF PICKLES, *continued*

place for a few days. Then go down and dig into the crock with a pair of long tongs, and pull yourself out one of the tastiest and simplest pickles around.

According to legend, Dad says, you should mix your water and salt solution to the point where a potato will float in the brine. He was kind of skeptical about this one, but you're going to have to experiment until you get your salt proportion right. Start a new crock every two weeks all summer. This is a great way to take advantage of all the bargains on pickling cucumbers at the farmers markets in August.

CUCUMBER SALAD

Strip peel 3 or 4 long cucumbers so that the peel is striped with alternating strips of bare cucumber. Next, slice the cucumbers into 1-inch slices and place in a large jar or bowl.

Combine marinade ingredients and add enough olive oil to cover cucumbers with liquid mixture. Place in refrigerator for two hours. Now, strain off the marinade and discard spices and lemon. To serve, add a can of pitted black olives and a can of pimento. Toss well and serve.

3–4 long cucumbers
3 cloves garlic, minced
1 cup cider vinegar
Juice and exhausted body of
   one lemon
¼ cup fresh dill or 3
   tablespoons dried
1 cup red wine
6 peppercorns
2 bay leaves
Olive oil

FRIED TOMATO SLICES

I was kind of skeptical about this dish until I tried it. The secret to its success lies in drying the tomato slices before dipping them. You can also use this recipe for frying eggplant. An especially colorful and delicious summer vegetable combination is fried eggplant with fried tomato, sprinkled with Parmesan cheese and fresh parsley. Alternate the slices and serve as accompaniment to fish or beef. It looks great and tastes even better.

Large tomatoes
Basil
Salt
Pepper
Vegetable oil
Corn meal or flour
Bread crumbs
Parmesan cheese, freshly grated

Slice tomatoes (you may want to peel them, but I don't) into ¼-inch slices. Lay out on paper towels. Place a second layer of paper towels on top of the tomatoes and pat lightly to absorb extra moisture. Sprinkle slices with basil, salt, and pepper.

Heat vegetable oil in a heavy skillet. Use just enough to cover tomato slices. Test temperature of oil by adding a drop of water. If the oil sizzles, it's ready.

Pick up each tomato slice with a fork. Be very careful. Dip into a shallow dish full of corn or wheat flour, then into a dish filled with milk to which the egg has been added. Finally, dip into a third dish filled with cracker or bread crumbs, making sure that each slice gets completely coated. Don't leave the tomatoes once you put them in the skillet. Watch them carefully and constantly readjust the flame so they cook quickly but don't burn. When they are golden, remove and drain on paper towels. Sprinkle with fresh Parmesan cheese and serve hot.

TOMATOES WITH BASIL AND SOUR CREAM

Slice large, beefsteak-style tomatoes horizontally, allowing to drain a little as you prepare other ingredients.

4 *large tomatoes*
2 *tablespoons butter*
4 *tablespoons fresh basil or*
   2 tablespoons dried
1 *cup sour cream*
Watercress
Hard-boiled eggs

Melt butter in a small skillet. Add basil and stir briskly, scraping sides of pan. Do not allow butter to brown or burn. Remove from heat and cool slightly.

Just before serving time, add 1 cup of sour cream to butter-basil mixture, and mix together. Spread sour cream mixture ¼-inch thick on top on tomato slices, garnish with watercress, and a slice of hard-boiled egg. For extra impact, stack tomato slices with layers of sour cream in between. You can devil the eggs, too, to get a red-white-yellow pattern. Good for a buffet where people serve themselves and have only themselves to blame for messing up the pretty picture.

DILLED BABY CORN

Stroll down the corn row and pick tiny ears of sweet corn when they are about 3 inches long. Check for tenderness by biting into the bottom end of the husked baby ears. If the inside is woody, throw away. Pack whole ears into quart Mason jars.

Baby ears of corn
1 *tablespoon salt*
1 *tablespoon sugar*
3 *garlic cloves*
1 *pinch alum*
1 *dill flower*
White vinegar

Prepare a mixture of salt, sugar, garlic, alum, and 1 dill flower per jar. Pour seasonings into the jar on top of the corn ears. Cover to fill with white vinegar to prevent discoloring of corn. Store in a cool, dry place. Check every 3 days and give jars a little shake to keep mixture in suspension.

After two weeks, ears should be well dilled.

CORN GRILLED IN HUSKS

Prepare your fire well ahead of time. Coals should be hot, but you don't have to be too picky. Just make sure that the fire has had a chance to work on the coals before you add the corn, and don't expect to rearrange or rebuild the fire after you have started to cook the corn.

Corn in husks, fresh
Plenty of butter, melted
  slowly

Check over the corn for worms and bugs. If it is good and healthy, prepare it for the meal. If it isn't, husk it and put it aside to cut out the bad parts and salvage what you can.

Pull the silk out of the top of the ear. You can pull the husk down all the way to the base on one side of the ear to get at the silk. Try to get out as much as you can.

Dribble the butter onto the exposed kernels on the open side of each ear. Don't worry about being too accurate, and don't worry if the butter gets on the husks. Then replace the husk so that it is rejoined at the top of the ear. Pat around the old wound, closing up the layers of the husk so that the buttered side is well protected.

Place the ears directly on the coals or else wrap each ear individually in aluminum foil. Use long tongs to turn the ears often. They should roast for about 18 to 25 minutes, depending on the intensity of the fire. Occasionally check on them by pricking a kernel with a fork to see how soft it is getting. Cook it to your personal preference.

GETTING YOUR COMMUNITY INVOLVED IN YOUR MARKET

Farmers markets serve as great a function in small towns in Minnesota as they do for the bustling population of a city like New York. They bring people fresh food, usually at lower prices; and regardless of the structure of the market it has the potential of becoming a center for community activity. The more activity a market has, the more customers. More customers attract more vendors with more variety of wares, and more profit and quality for all involved.

Community involvement benefits both people and the market itself. The market needs to attract people, and a community needs a market. But it is usually only a small percent of the community that makes the effort to shop at a farmers market on a given day at a given time. The other people may mean to shop there, but the convenience of the supermarket may be too attractive to them. The market management has to find a way to bring those people to the market. Once there, they'll be hooked. But how do you get them there?

Many communities have service organizations or school groups that have a full calendar of activities. A first step toward involving some of these people would be to send a representative of the market to meet with those groups to discuss how the market works, and how the facility can be useful to the groups. If the vendors are members of the community, it may be easy to accomplish this.

Service groups need to raise money to perform their services, and sometimes those services need a place to happen. A carwash in the parking lot of the farmers market on a Saturday morning will bring out all the parents of the carwashers, and more people as well. A hospital service group might want to have a bake sale. Or the Girl Scouts might want to sell cookies. The 4-H might need a forum for a sheep-shearing demonstration. A local theater group or puppet troupe might like a place to give a sample show. If you can open up the market to groups like these you are beginning to really serve a community function, and will be on the way to entrenching the market in the community's tradition.

FRIED PUMPKIN BLOSSOMS

A farmers market vendor who offers pumpkin or squash blossoms to shoppers is a thinking gardener. Pinching the blossoms helps the plants concentrate growth on selected produce, and at the same time, makes a delicious treat. The blossoms should be picked just before they open. Pick through the blossoms carefully—they injure easily—and select some that are swollen but still shut.

Arrange the blossoms on a large sheet of wax paper or a pastry sheet. Top with an equal-sized sheet of wax paper and put a weight on top of the blossoms to flatten them. Leave them with the weight on for about 5 minutes.

Dip the flattened blossoms in a mixture of the beaten egg and milk. Then roll the blossoms in a mixture of the bread crumbs and sesame seeds.

Deep fry the blossoms in reserved bacon fat or cooking oil. Serve very hot, sprinkled with dill and freshly ground pepper.

Pumpkin blossoms
1 egg, beaten
2 tablespoons milk
¼ cup dry bread crumbs
¼ cup sesame seeds
Bacon fat or cooking oil
Dill
Pepper

ZUCCHINI MIKONOS

Sauté zucchini and garlic in olive oil until zucchini is coated with oil and begins to soften. Then add the rest of the ingredients and cook, stirring often, over medium heat until mixture begins to bubble. Simmer for 5 to 10 minutes or until zucchini is limp and tender. Transfer to an earthenware bowl and let cool to room temperature. Refrigerate before serving, preferably overnight. Just before serving, add red onion rings and toss until rings are coated with liquid. Discard bay leaf and drain off excess liquid. Serve as a side dish for a cold meal.

4 medium zucchini, 5–7
*   inches each, slice in*
*   ¼-inch slices*
⅓ cup olive oil
1 cup white wine
½ cup dried parsley
1 teaspoon fresh thyme
2 tablespoons lemon juice
1 teaspoon dried tarragon
1 garlic clove, chopped
1 bay leaf
2 tablespoons butter
1 cup red onion rings

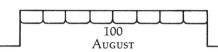

SKEWERED SWORDFISH

Swordfish is one of my favorite foods. It really is a shame that it is so expensive and so hard to get in most supermarkets. It is definitely worth the trek to a fish market, however. It is a filling food, so estimate a little less than you would for a lighter fish. Swordfish is dense.

Most people will eat swordfish even if they don't like fish. This characteristic makes it a good choice for guests, particularly vegetarian guests who do not eat meat. The real problem may be that buying enough swordfish for 3 or 4 or (heaven forbid!) 6 people can cost a week's salary. Hence, this recipe.

I didn't invent this recipe, and I won't pretend I did. For years, this was the only way I ever ate swordfish, because this is the way that so many restaurants serve it, calling it "en brochette." If you ever figured out the price per pound of the swordfish you order in a restaurant this way, you'd be horrified.

So why should restaurants be able to get away with it? Join the pack. Serve your guests food that they and you will love, food that will be colorful, nutritious, and different. And if they don't like swordfish, they can have skewered vegetables!

This recipe will make about 8 skewers. Depending on how generous you want to be with the swordfish, you can condense it to six, and have some vegetables left over. It's up to you. It's also nice to have some extra vegetables when you start assembling the skewers. If your dinners are anything like mine, there often turn out to be more guests than you had planned on, and the swordfish can go a lot farther with a few padded vegetables here and there.

2 pounds swordfish
Soy sauce
White wine
Lemon juice
1 pint ripe cherry tomatoes
2 large green peppers, seeds removed, and cut in chunks
2 dozen large white mushrooms
2 medium zucchini, cut in ½-inch slices
Lemon

SKEWERED SWORDFISH, *continued*

By the way, if any of your guests ask for this recipe, don't give it to them. Make them think that it really was a major project and that you learned it from a chef under torture. With any luck they'll believe you, and your swordfish will become legendary.

Several hours before you plan to serve this wonderful meal, cut the swordfish into 1-inch chunks. Put the chucks in a glass dish and pour over them the marinade: 3 parts soy sauce, 2 parts white wine, and 1 part lemon juice. Be generous. See to it that all the pieces are at least partially submerged in the marinade. Cover and place in refrigerator. If it is winter, and you have a cool pantry and a cat you can trust, leave it out because it will marinate better. Just make sure that it is not near any heat source.

The afternoon of the day you plan to serve this dish, turn fish chunks so that the formerly unsubmerged sides of your fish chunks are now in the liquid. Replace cover and leave alone.

About one hour before dinner, begin to assemble the parts; place vegetable and fish chunks in alternating patterns on the skewers. Push them tightly together so they will help support each other as they cook and soften.

Line broiler pan with aluminum foil. Pour marinade over each skewer, making sure to coat well. Broil 2 to 3 minutes on each side, basting with marinade as you go. Heat remaining marinade and pour into a small pitcher to serve as a sauce, with a sliced lemon in the pitcher for decoration and added flavor. Serve fish kebabs on a bed of rice.

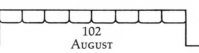

MJEDDRAH

What did you say? This dish is unpronounceable. Call it what you like; it's a cold vegetable casserole of Middle-Eastern origin. Sonja, a long-lost cooking friend, taught me this one. Sonja was a redhead with a heart of gold, and this exotic tasting midsummer dinner treat is as much fun to make and eat as it can be. Just be careful—when Sonja gave me this recipe, she gave me restaurant proportions. This is enough for about ten people. Make it for a party; people will love it. Every bite is a surprise.

Sauté the onion in the olive oil. When it starts to soften, add the green pepper, garlic, oregano, coriander, and cumin and sauté, stirring until uniformly softened and onion turns lightly golden. Add rice and lentils and 6 cups of water. Cover and cook at least one hour.

Slice zucchini and cucumber and marinate them in tamari, dill, and red wine vinegar while rice and lentils are cooking. When rice and lentils are softened, stir well to distribute seasonings, onion, and green pepper throughout.

Cover the bottom of a serving platter with the zucchini and cucumbers. Cover with cooled lentil and rice mixture, forming a mound. Spoon cottage cheese on top and top with wedges of tomato. Refrigerate for an hour or so before serving, sliced into wedges.

2 *green peppers, sliced*
2 *onions, sliced*
1 *tablespoon minced garlic*
½ *teaspoon oregano*
½ *tablespoon coriander (ground)*
1 *tablespoon cumin*
2 *cups brown or white rice*
3½ *cups lentils*
2 *sliced cucumbers*
1 *sliced medium zucchini*
1 *cup tamari*
½ *cup red wine vinegar*
1 *tablespoon dill weed*
1 *pint cottage cheese*
2 *tomatoes, cut into wedges*
⅓ *cup olive oil*

MELONS

I wish that I knew how to buy melons. I wish that I could cut open a melon without holding my breath and crossing my fingers. Sometimes I buy the split-open cantaloupes at the "reduced for quick sale" counter at the supermarket just to avoid the dilemma of buying melons at the outdoor market out of season. As long as you eat them the same day you buy them, these discount melons are usually fine for eating—and a bargain besides. Just look carefully at them before you buy them. Soft, darker orange spots are signs of extreme age. And white mold on the rind says that it's too late for eating that one.

Of course, there is a logical way to tell a melon's age and relative ripeness. Melons are an "intelligent" fruit; when allowed to stay on the vine, they signal their parent plant when ripe. The parent plant shrivels up the cord of life to that particular melon. When you walk through the melon patch, you merely pick the melons with shriveled life vines to the parent vine. A little scar tissue grows at the end of the ripe melon where the vine was.

That's fine if it's August and you have them in your garden. But if they've been on a truck for three days and the kid at the stand is yelling at you to quit picking at the melons . . . what are you going to do?

A lot of the melons I see at the market are cut off where the little scar should be. Melons can't ripen after they're picked, so it seems to me that Americans eat a lot of unripe melons.

My father is adept at knocking on melons to ascertain their ripeness—by a hollow sound rather than a deadened thud. If you are one of those lucky individuals who has a knack for knocking, I envy you. I always knock—for good luck, I guess—but I'm never able to remember what the "right" knock should sound like. They all sound ripe to me. And someday the guy at the pushcart is going to wallop me for knocking his melons!

Melons are generally available from May through September. Unless you live in the West or Southwest, you are really taking a chance to buy a melon in February. Besides, they're worth waiting for!

CARROT SHERBET

This cool, refreshing treat will make everyone guess what the flavor is. This is an easy, elegant dessert for hot summer nights.

1 quart fresh carrot juice
2 ounces Triple Sec liqueur
1 6-ounce can of frozen
    lemonade concentrate
Dash of grenadine syrup
¼ cup superfine sugar
1 whole banana, cut up

Combine all the ingredients in a blender and blend at medium speed. Keep the top off the blender and watch the mixture until you have a smoothly flowing liquid. Turn the blender off immediately. Pour the liquid into a mold or use ice cube trays. Freeze, stirring occasionally to get proper consistency when done. Serve as a dessert with yogurt that has been flavored with a tablespoon of orange juice concentrate and a teaspoon of sugar.

WILD BLACKBERRY PIE

Prepare a basic pie crust recipe and put bottom crust into 9-inch pie pan. Prick bottom with a fork.

4 cups wild blackberries
1 teaspoon nutmeg
1 tablespoon flour
1 tablespoon butter
Pie crust
Egg white
Sugar

Set aside a handful of berries. Mix rest of the blackberries with the flour, nutmeg, and butter. Pour into pie pan and sprinkle sugar over berries.

Add top crust, either as one piece or lattice-style. Crimp edges to seal. Brush top crust with beaten egg white and sprinkle more sugar on top.

Bake for 45 minutes at 400°. Serve with vanilla ice cream, à la mode fashion. Garnish ice cream with reserved berries.

NEWCOMBVILLE GRANGE BAKE SALE

SEPTEMBER

★Meet Me at the Fair★
Hot Dogs in Bacon
Turkey Legs a la Flash
Taco Madness Hot Sauce
Blue Ribbon Brownies
Fresh Chutney
Marinated Carrots, Broccoli,
and Cauliflower
Sauerkraut
Rose Hip Jam

Bean Salad
Eastern Carrots
Ratatouille
Homemade Potato Chips
Kookala (Potato Souffle)
Basic Applesauce
Applesauce Cake
Penuche Frosting
Grandpa's Shortcake
Whipped Cream Topping

MEET ME AT THE FAIR

Have you ever wanted to be one of those carefree, slightly crazy people who sell food on the midway at a state or country fair? The sounds, the smells —they're mesmerizing, aren't they? And then you enter the coolness of the exhibit halls and pass through aisles and aisles flanked with tier upon tier of the biggest pumpkins, best decorated cakes, best jams and jellies, most authentic apple pies—the scene is awesome. Those people must work all year to produce these prize winners. And the vendors outside are lining their pockets.

When it comes to country fairs, I'm hooked. Every fall, my lawn goes unraked because every weekend finds me off to a different fair. I've never seen a fair that I didn't like, and every one is better than the one before; but the World's Fair in Tunbridge, Vermont is probably the best there is anywhere.

I've been on both ends of the food world at country fairs. I've won ribbons for baking and ribbons for vegetables (lost a lot of ribbons too), and I've been a longstanding vendor out on the midway with the hawkers and the strippers. If you've got a secret dream to be on the midway or to put your food up against the champions, do it this year. There's nothing like a country fair, especially when you are part of it.

Until I met Kathy and Merle Schloff, country fairs meant hanging on the fence at the horse pulls and standing in line at the beerhalls. Then in 1974 Kathy and Merle came to me with the idea of starting a new food tradition at the World's Fair. We've been in business at Taco Madness ever since.

Taco Madness started out with my old drafting table, a pile of Suzanne's aprons, a rolling pin, and the help of everybody we could pull in. We opened a taco stand that was so pure that people stopped in the middle of the midway just to watch us work. We made our own tortillas by hand and rolled each one out, to order. We cut each vegetable up by hand and used lean ground beef—no beans—for the filling. We had no plumbing, no roof, and no end to the line of customers. And we've been in the same spot ever since.

Almost ten years later, Taco Madness is still going strong. We're a little more profitable now, although we do work hard to keep the prices down. This year we had to install running water—every year the health department seems to come up with a new regulation for us to meet. But we're still there, across from the ferris wheel, next to the vegetable display hall, and we have no intention of leaving.

The biggest reason for sticking it out on the midway is the friends that we have there. We see them once a year, but for four days, once a year, we are family: The bizarre Flash and his friends from the turkey legs stand (they have no electricity and advertise candle-light dining for you and your loved one), the three-legged dog from the roast corn stand, the con men from the

MEET ME AT THE FAIR

gambling stand, and the hot-dog-wrapped-in-bacon man who always will trade a taco for his wonderful hot dogs. I don't know what any of those people do during the rest of the year, and I don't ask. For those days, we are carnies together; we complain that the crowd isn't buying, that this is the worst year in Tunbridge history, that the health department was never so strict before, that we are losing our shirts—and, as the last tent flap falls, that we will see each other next year.

HOT DOGS WRAPPED IN BACON

Roll each hot dog in a long strip of bacon and grill over charcoal until the bacon is crisp. Garnish with sauerkraut, chili, barbecue sauce, mustard, relish, catsup—whatever your heart desires.

TURKEY LEGS À LA FLASH

No one knows for sure what Flash puts in his turkey legs, or rather, what he puts his turkey legs in. It's probably, plain and simple, a dose of pure magic. To recreate a country fair turkey leg in the comfort of your own home, marinate each leg (1 per person) in a jug of red wine, and baste with melted butter as the legs roast over charcoal. For atmosphere, play the Rolling Stones at full blast, and invite a motorcycle gang over for a good gnaw. Hard to beat.

TACO MADNESS HOT SAUCE

"Hey, hot stuff here!" Nick Theopolis of Derby, Connecticut didn't think that our peppers were so hot last year. In the world championship jalapeno pepper eating contest at our Taco Madness stand, Nick ate 74 jalapeno peppers in less than an hour, without anything else to eat or drink. He probably eats our hot sauce on his breakfast cereal.

Fresh overripe tomatoes
Olive oil
Cider vinegar
Garlic powder
Sugar
Jalapeno peppers
Onion

To prepare our sauce, almost fill a blender container with fresh, overripe tomatoes. Add ½ cup olive oil and ¼ cup cider vinegar. Toss in a tablespoon of garlic powder and ¼ cup of sugar. Last, add 2 jalapeno peppers. Blend at high speed. Pour off 1 cup of the sauce and mark this "mild." To the rest of the blender ingredients, add another 2 jalapenos. Pour off a cup and mark this "not so mild." Then add 2 more jalapeno peppers to the remaining ingredients. Continue, in this fashion, until you get to the bottom of the blender. Then add a small onion and a handful of jalapeno peppers and a little more oil and vinegar. Turn on the blender and make a relish-like mixture. Scrape this into a bowl and mark this "too hot."

Try not to touch the peppers with your fingers. If you do, wash your hands right away. *Don't rub your eyes!!* They really do burn. I've seen skin peel off people's hands, and I wouldn't like to see the lining of Nick Theopolis's stomach. Although, just maybe, it's lined with cast iron . . .

BLUE RIBBON BROWNIES

Here it is, the one you've been waiting for. The perennial choice of the Bolton, Massachusetts Fair is here for all to bake. Just be sure to make a lot more than you need—they'll be gone before you know it.

By the way, this is my mother's recipe. All the credit goes to her. Almond extract and cream cheese are the secret.

Melt chocolate with butter. It's best to float a stainless steel measuring cup with the ingredients in a pan of boiling water so that the chocolate doesn't burn. While the chocolate is melting, sift together the flour, baking powder, and salt. In another bowl, beat the eggs. Gradually add 1 cup sugar. The butter and chocolate should be melted by now; cool slightly. Add vanilla and butter and chocolate to the eggs. Add dry ingredients and mix well.

Spread the brownie mixture in a greased 9-by-13-inch baking pan. It will be very thick; spread it out with a sturdy spatula, being careful to get the batter into the corners of the pan.

You can prepare the topping batter in the blender. Just pour everything in and blend until smooth. Pour the almond–cream cheese mixture into the pan with the chocolate mixture and marble with a knife.

Bake at 350° for 45 minutes. Brownies are done when the top springs back to your touch, and a broom straw comes out clean. Let cool completely before you cut them.

For proper effect, deliver these brownies to your fair one minute before entries close so that no one else sees the "secret" brownies until there's a blue ribbon hanging on them.

2 squares unsweetened chocolate
⅓ cup butter
⅔ cup unsifted flour
½ teaspoon baking power
¼ teaspoon salt
2 eggs
1 cup sugar
1 teaspoon vanilla

Topping

8 ounces cream cheese
⅓ cup sugar
1 teaspoon almond extract
1 egg

FRESH CHUTNEY

Combine ingredients with enough yogurt to reach desired consistency. Store chutney in a sealed container in a refrigerator, and use it as an accompaniment to all kinds of cold or hot meals. Once you have learned to appreciate it, begin to experiment with the ingredients, and make your own formula. You can also make more exotic Eastern chutneys with curry and mango and coconut, but this native version is just fine with me.

½ cup grated carrot
½ cup diced cucumber
½ cup diced onion
1 tablespoon fresh lime juice
1 tablespoon dried parsley
1 teaspoon grated fresh
    ginger

MARINATED CARROTS, BROCCOLI, AND CAULIFLOWER

Bring all the marinade ingredients except lemon juice to a boil and remove from heat. Add lemon juice and stir well.

In a large glass jar or salad bowl, arrange the vegetables in layers by colors. Use a thin layer of onions between broccoli and carrots. Stud cauliflower and carrot layers with parsley sprigs that are visible from the outside. Then pour marinade over all and cover. Marinate at room temperature or in a refrigerator for at least 8 hours before serving. Have pepper mill on the table for seasoning.

1 small head cauliflower,
    broken into tiny flowers
1 head broccoli, cut into
    flowerets
2 pounds of carrots, sliced
2 small onions, diced
Several sprigs of fresh parsley

Marinade

½ cup sugar
½ cup white wine vinegar
½ cup olive oil
¼ cup lemon juice

SAUERKRAUT

Sauerkraut is best made in a large crock and then canned for a long season of enjoyment. (Have you ever had a glass of sauerkraut juice?) For the impatient, here is a stove-top recipe for sauerkraut that you can make when the mood hits. And why not encourage a market vendor to sell sauerkraut?

1 quart sauerkraut
½ cup granulated sugar
2 medium onions, diced
1 tablespoon vinegar
1 apple, peeled and diced
1 tablespoon butter

Combine all the ingredients except for the butter and one of the onions. Pour water over all the ingredients and cook for at least 30 minutes.

Brown the second onion in the butter. Add it to the mixture when the cooking time is up. Serve immediately for hot kraut, or refrigerate and serve as part of a cold buffet.

ROSE HIP JAM

Rose hips are the highest concentrated source of Vitamin C available in nature. Rose hips can be gathered in the wild wherever wild roses grow. The shore is the most plentiful source, but look also in overgrown meadows. For best cooking results, gather rose hips right after the first frost.

1 pound rose hips
1 cup water
1 pound sugar

Simmer washed rose hips in water until they are tender. Rub them through a sieve and weigh the pulp. To each pound of pulp, add 1 pound of sugar. Reheat pulp with sugar and simmer until it thickens. Stir often. Seal in hot, sterilized jars.

BEAN SALAD

Every summer buffet has to have a bean salad, and if it's your turn to make it, why not make it the best?

Fill serving bowl with green peppers, onions, cut-up green and yellow wax beans, lima beans, and kidney beans.

Put all the dressing ingredients (except olive oil) in a saucepan, and bring them to a boil. Add olive oil, and bring to a boil again. Pour dressing over bean mixture, and allow to marinate for a few hours before serving.

Green peppers, sliced
Red onions, thinly sliced into rings
Green beans
Yellow wax beans
Fresh or frozen lima beans
Canned kidney beans

Dressing

¾ *cup sugar*
⅔ *cup red wine vinegar*
1 *teaspoon salt*
1 *teaspoon pepper*
¾ *teaspoon celery seed*
2 *tablespoons Pommery mustard*
⅓ *cup olive oil*

EASTERN CARROTS

Steam peeled carrots until they are fork-tender. Melt butter over low heat in a shallow, wide pan and add the carrots, spooning butter over them.

In a small bowl mix together brown sugar, sesame oil, and dark soy sauce. Pour it over the carrots. Cook the carrots over low heat, but hot enough to keep the butter bubbly. Turn the carrots, cooking them until they are evenly browned.

12 *carrots, tops removed*
¼ *cup butter*
¼ *cup brown sugar*
¼ *cup sesame oil*
3 *tablespoons dark soy sauce*

RATATOUILLE

You can serve ratatouille as a cold side dish in the summer or as a hearty main dish in the winter. Either way you serve it, it's still fun to say it. This is a great dish for winter months when leafy, fresh vegetables are scarce, but there's a special taste to ratatouille made from garden-fresh vegetables straight from the farmers market. Keep an eye out for a dealer with the kind of eggplants that make your heart ache because they're so beautifully purple. In the north, wait until the end of the summer season. Eggplant needs a long growing season.

Heat oil and butter in large, deep-sided frying pan or Dutch oven. When heated, add minced garlic and onion, and stir until onion turns golden and limp. Add green peppers, stir for a minute and add zucchini, eggplant and tomatoes. Simmer for about 5 minutes, stirring to make sure that everything is well coated with oil and butter mixture. Pour in red wine and tomato paste, sprinkle with oregano, and cover. Lift cover occasionally and give ingredients a good stir. Simmer covered for 30 to 60 minutes, depending on how mushy you like your ratatouille. Also, whether you used fresh or canned tomatoes will make a difference. The canned tomatoes will make the dish more souplike. Keep an eye on the tomatoes, and when they are the way you like them remove the pan from heat. Let cool for an hour or more. When room temperature, add breadcrumbs and toss, making sure that they become well mixed. At this point, transfer to serving dish or refrigerate for serving later. Before serving, garnish with lemon slices and freshly ground black pepper.

2 *medium zucchini, cut in 1-inch chunks*

1 *eggplant, peeled and cut in 1-inch chunks*

2 *medium green peppers, cored, seeded, and cut in squares*

1 *can of Italian tomatoes* or 4 *large fresh peeled tomatoes, cut in chunks*

2 *medium onions, cut up*

½ *cup olive oil*

¼ *cup butter*

¼ *cup red wine*

2 *cloves minced garlic*

1 *teaspoon oregano*

2 *cups fresh breadcrumbs, toasted*

2 *tablespoons tomato paste*

1 *lemon*

HOMEMADE POTATO CHIPS

Slice washed, peeled potatoes thinly (⅛- to ¼-inch thick) into a waiting bowl of cold water.

Line several shallow, rectangular baking pans with aluminum foil and preheat oven to 350°. You may also use teflon-coated pans, if you have them. The aluminum foil just prevents the potatoes from sticking.

Pour about ⅛ inch oil into each pan and put them in the oven. Watch through the oven window or open door occasionally to check on pans. When the oil is heated and just beginning to smoke, pull the pans out of the oven with potholders.

Drop the potato slices by handfuls into the hot oil. Bake the potato slices for 3 to 4 minutes or until lightly coated. Pull from heat quickly, flip over potato slices, and return to heat for another minute or until oil begins to sizzle again.

Next move the potatoes from the oil and onto racks, absorbent paper towels, or brown paper bags for draining. You may also drain off the oil, then pour potatoes into brown paper bags and shake to absorb oil into paper.

Let the potato slices cool. Meanwhile, raise the heat in the oven to broil.

When the broiler is heated, lay the potatoes in the shallow pans again. This is where the aluminum foil comes in handy. Pass the pans under the boiler. Shake or flip so that both sides feel the broiler's heat.

Drain off any excess moisture from the pans and blot potato slices dry. When cool, add salt and shake in individual bags or a jar.

For a special treat, you can make your potato slices "taco flavored." Mix together chili powder,

Potatoes
Vegetable oil
Salt

Taco flavoring

1 *tablespoon chili powder*
1 *tablespoon cumin*
1 *tablespoon salt*
2 *tablespoons grated
      Parmesan cheese*

HOMEMADE POTATO CHIPS, *continued*

cumin, salt, and add grated Parmesan cheese. Sprinkle this mixture over the still moist broiled slices and let them dry with the mixture on them or run them under the broiler again.

KOOKALA (POTATO SOUFFLE)

Cut up ham, bacon, or salt pork and fry with onion. Stir as they cook until the onion is slightly brown. Set these ingredients aside.

Peel and grate the potatoes quickly (you can grate them into a cup or so of milk to prevent discoloring; just remember to drain the milk before going on to the next step). Mix potatoes, onion, and meat together, and add the milk and beaten eggs. Add salt and pepper, and stir in the flour.

Pour the batter into a 9-by-13-inch pan. Dot the top with butter. Bake for 1½ to 2 hours at 375°. Serve with a sour cream garnish.

¾ cup chopped bacon, salt pork or leftover ham
12 large potatoes
1 large onion, chopped
½ cup milk
2 eggs, beaten
Salt and pepper, to taste
¼ cup flour

BASIC APPLESAUCE

Put apples and water in a pot. Cover tightly and cook over medium heat for 20 minutes. Add sugar and stir briskly. Cook for one more minute, then remove from heat. Whip with a wooden spoon. Spread some warm applesauce on a slice of homemade bread, and refrigerate the rest. Just before serving, sprinkle with cinnamon.

6–8 tart apples, cut up
½ cup water
½ cup sugar
Cinnamon, to taste

APPLESAUCE CAKE

Cream butter and sugar. Add eggs and beat well.

Sift together flour and spices. Gradually blend into creamed mixture. Then mix baking soda into applesauce and add to batter. Pour into greased and floured 9-by-13-inch pan and bake at 350° for 50 to 60 minutes. When cake is cool, frost with penuche frosting.

1½ cups brown sugar,
    packed
1 cup butter
2 eggs
2 teaspoons baking soda
2 cups thick unsweetened
    applesauce
3 cups flour
½ teaspoon salt
1 teaspoon ground cloves
2 teaspoons cinnamon
¼ teaspoon ground ginger
¾ cups chopped nuts

PENUCHE FROSTING

Mix ingredients in a heavy saucepan. Stir over low heat to melt sugar, then bring to a full boil stirring constantly.

Boil for exactly 1 minute. Remove from heat and beat until lukewarm or of spreading consistency.

2 cups light brown sugar,
    packed
½ cup milk
½ cup butter
¼ teaspoon salt

GRANDPA'S SHORTCAKE

The grandpa in this recipe belongs to Molly Price. Molly is one of those people who can bake and cook with the greatest of ease, and I have learned a lot from her. I've lost track of Molly, but I salute her and her grandpa with this, her recipe.

Sift together flour, baking powder, and salt. Add the dry ingredients to the softened butter, which has been mixed with the egg and milk.

Pour into two 8-inch round baking pans that have been greased and floured. Bake at 450° for 15 minutes. Serve with sliced peaches and whipped cream topping.

2 cups flour
3 teaspoons baking powder
½ teaspoon salt
2½ tablespoons butter,
    softened
1 egg
¾ cup milk

WHIPPED CREAM TOPPING FOR FRESH FRUIT

Add maple syrup or 1 tablespoon of one of the alternatives to cream before whipping.

Top off whipped cream and fruit with slivered almonds, ground walnuts, chunks of Gourmandaise dessert cheese or a dribble of Créme de Cassis.

1 pint heavy cream
1 tablespoon maple syrup

Alternatives

Amaretto liqueur
Grand Marnier liqueur
Curacao liqueur
Honey (1 tablespoon plus 1
    teaspoon lemon juice)

OCTOBER

★ What Makes a Market Great? ★
Country Lentil Stew
★ Roast Pig Perfection ★
Barbecue Sauce for Roast Pig
★ Ham ★
Cider Boiled Ham Dinner

Apple Baked Ham Roast
Baked Apples
★ Horseradish ★
Capellini with Meat Sauce
Pesto for Pasta
Pasta Buffet
Halloween Sweet Treats

WHAT MAKES A GOOD FARMERS MARKET GREAT?

● A playground for children to play in while parents shop. Even a play area, with some sort of fence and a supervisor, will help. Vendors can bring their children to this area while the parents are selling, and the children of buyers will look forward to going to the farmers market for the play area. Why haven't supermarkets ever done this?

● Recipe demonstrations by vendor/chefs of rare or plentiful produce to encourage sales. Trying different recipes out on passing customers will increase their awareness of produce and make them remember the vendor. Printed recipes of the dish will help spur sales, too. Check with your local health department concerning regulations about cooking and serving food.

● Displays of how the produce is grown will help business. If the vendors are also growers and they live in the area, so much the better. Customers will enjoy meeting a grower who lives in the same area, and will be interested to know that a half-acre yields enough zucchini to support an industry. Beyond education, make the market a show. Bring in a milking goat, and demonstrate the differences between goat's and cow's milk, both in technique and in nutritional and flavor content. Baby animals are always popular with families, so try to make sure that each week has a different display: baby pigs with their mom (for sale!) one week, goats the next, chickens the next. The word will get around.

● Somewhere on the grounds of your market, have a space set aside for picnicking. Offer to sell produce like melons all cut up for people to munch on, and you'll sell more, expecially if there is a shady tree, a trash barrel, and a picnic table nearby.

COUNTRY LENTIL STEW

This recipe was passed along to me many years ago; I know not whence it came. If it's your recipe, thank you. It's a great stew, and I don't have any pretentions of having come up with this recipe. Just enjoy it—and pass it along.

2 cups dry lentils
¼ pound salt pork
Salt and pepper to taste
1 onion, chopped
1 cup chopped celery
½ teaspoon thyme
1 bay leaf
½ teaspoon sugar
2 tablespoons butter
2 tablespoons flour
Juice of one lemon
1 lemon, sliced

Begin by soaking lentils overnight in a bowl with at least one inch of cold water covering them. When you get up the next morning, drain off the water.

Put the lentils in a large saucepan with 9 cups of water and the salt pork. Add some salt and pepper; go easy on the salt. Heat thoroughly and bring to a boil. Simmer for 3 hours.

Then add the onion, celery, thyme, bay leaf, and sugar, and simmer for 30 minutes more. At that time, pull out the salt pork and the bay leaf—their work is done.

Start running the soup through an electric blender set on "puree." Continue until entire contents of the saucepan have been blended.

Melt the butter in a small frying pan and add the flour. Stir them together to make a roux. Use a whisk. When the roux is thick, add one cup of the soup. Beat rapidly with the whisk.

Stir this cupful back into the main pot of soup. Then increase the heat and bring the soup to a boil again. Simmer 10 minutes.

Just before serving, add the lemon juice. Serve very hot with lemon slices as garnish.

PIG ROAST PERFECTION

A pig roast is a wonderful excuse to have a party. And with more and more people experimenting with raising their own pigs, the rite of a pig roast is getting to be more popular.

If you don't have a young boar to sacrifice, but you would still like to invite a few dozen friends and neighbors over for a pig roast (don't forget the neighbors, because the smell of roast pig will drive their salivary glands crazy), go ahead and give it a try. Go to your local slaughterhouse or, if you live in the city, inquire at a specialty butcher shop about pigs for roasting.

A pig roast is not for the neophyte. Find someone who has done it before and get help. You must begin preparations several days in advance, aside from finding and ordering a pig. You need lots of firewood, lots of space for people, and a pit. Do not enter into this endeavor lightly. If you just want to have a pig roast, call a caterer who specializes in them. Leave the hard work to them.

Directions are not given here for slaughtering a pig; no one should attempt to slaughter a pig with one hand, and hold a cookbook in the other. Again, find someone who is experienced. Or take your pig to a slaughterhouse, and ask them to dress it out for a split pig roast.

Build a hot fire in the pit. Make sure that you have plenty of fuel. Split the pig, back up, so it lies flat on the grill. The grill can be any sort of metal laid over the fire to support the pig. You can use a wrought iron fence section, some pipes with metal mesh wire fence over it, or whatever you have. Cook the pig in this way for three hours, then turn on its back.

Pour ½ gallon of barbecue sauce into the inside of the pig, and cook for another 5 hours. Periodically, add more sauce, and brush with a paintbrush. Keep an eye on the fire, making sure that you still have plenty of fuel.

Fat will be dripping regularly down into the coals, and that will keep the fire going at a hot sizzle. The meat on the back will be ready after 8 hours, but some other parts may need another 2 hours, like the shoulders and hams.

Test the meat for doneness by pulling at joints and twisting. When the meat is easily pulled (much like chicken), it is done. *At no time allow the pig to burn.* Keep an eye on the fire.

Remove skin and cut the meat from the bones.

BARBECUE SAUCE FOR ROAST PIG

Combine ingredients, and simmer for 30 minutes, stirring often. Makes one gallon, enough for an average sized pig.

2 14-ounce bottles of catsup
2 14-ounce bottles of chili sauce
1 8-ounce bottle red wine vinegar
Juice of three lemons, plus squeezed lemon bodies
1 4-ounce jar of Dijon-style mustard
1 8-ounce jar Worcestershire sauce
2 1½-ounce jars crushed red peppers
Salt and pepper, to taste

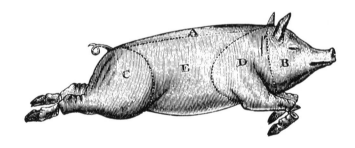

HAM

You'll be very lucky if you can find a farmers market with a butcher shop that offers fine hams. Try one, if you can. Fine hams are also available by mail order, or else raise your own pig and eat homemade ham. Chances are, though, that for economy and convenience you will end up buying a ham at a supermarket. Whenever I go to a supermarket to buy a ham, it seems like there's a new kind that I've never seen before, and I forget what kind I set out to buy. It is confusing.

What is the difference between a picnic shoulder and a shank end? Should you buy bone in or bone out? What about the hams that are rolled into shapes that bear no resemblance to any part of any pig you ever saw? What does "water added" mean? Cooked? Uncooked?

First off, the "real" kind of ham, in supermarket lingo, is a smoked country ham. They are available as butt or shank ends. They will be the leanest and the best for a main course. You can also get a picnic shoulder, which means that it comes from the foreleg of the pig instead of the more traditional hind leg. It is apt to be riddled with fatty deposits, though, and won't be as impressive on the table or nearly as economical.

Ham shrinks up during the curing process, so water is routinely added to restore mass to the meat. Depending on the process, timing, and the meat itself, it may be necessary to add a lot more water to some hams than to others. If the ham's label says "water added," it indicates that up to 10 percent of the total weight of the ham you are buying is added water. No marking at all indicates that the water is a minute quantity making it simply a "ham." If the label or packaging says "imitation," there is more than 10 percent water inside the meat.

Boneless hams are more economical, since you are buying meat by the pound, but they are less flavorful than the bone-in style. Most hams available in markets are precooked, and may say "ready to eat." They may well be, but do yourself—and your guests—a favor and bake the ham with some sort of sauce or basting to improve the flavor.

If you find yourself with a country ham on your hands, prepare it a day before serving by thoroughly scrubbing on the outside for any residue of salt or mold, then soak overnight in cider or just plain water. You must boil the ham for several hours after soaking, and then bake it. Follow the instructions from step 1 in the recipes from this book for a supermarket "ready to eat" ham. For a country ham, consult your butcher for cleaning and preparation suggestions for the particular ham in question, and then cook with one of the recipes here.

CIDER BOILED HAM DINNER

Select a smoked shoulder that will fit nicely into a small kettle. Thinking ahead, you might want to plan to make an apple pie for dessert with this meal.

Smoked shoulder ham
Apple cider
Apples
Whole cloves
1 cup maple syrup
Carrots, peeled and cut into
    strips

Place the smoked shoulder in the kettle and cover halfway with water. Fill to almost covered with good cider, an old New England remedy for too-salty ham.

As you peel apples to make the pie, reserve the peelings. When finished, put these peelings into the pot with the ham. Boil ham gently for one hour.

Remove ham from liquid. On a draining board, slice away the protective fat side of the shoulder, leaving a layer of fat around the end of the bone. Score the ham with diagonal cuts with a sharp knife, and stud it with whole cloves.

With a large fork, lift the shoulder into a shallow baking pan (about 2 inches high is a good size). Mix together one cup of maple syrup (B grade is best) with one cup of apple cider, and pour it slowly over the shoulder. If you are careful, you can get the liquid to run right through the cross cuts, insuring good flavoring of the meat.

With the oven pre-set at 425°, place the ham in the middle of the oven for about 40 minutes. Then reduce the heat to 350° and bake about 20 minutes per pound. Baste every ten minutes or so.

In the last half hour of cooking, add peeled carrot strips to the base of the shoulder, spooning sauce over the carrots as you add them. Serve the carrots with the ham.

Baked apples are good as a side dish to this ham instead of a dessert.

APPLE BAKED HAM ROAST

I have seen and tasted many variations of this traditional fall dinner. Ham is not a uniform-tasting meat, so it is likely that your rendition of this recipe will never taste the same twice.

Ham
Cider
½ cup maple syrup
Raisins

Well, if you have a smoked ham from your own pig, you're going to have to boil it first, so you might as well try adding some cider to the water. Boil ham for 15 minutes per pound. If you are buying a ham from the supermarket, chances are that you have a pre-cooked ham that says "ready to eat" on it. It is already boiled, but it will taste a whole lot better when we're through baking it.

After boiling, or after removing plastic from pre-cooked variety, cut away the thick fat that surrounds the ham, except for the bone at the end (if it has a bone). Leave a good-sized strip there. Put ham in a shallow roasting pan, and dribble over it a sauce made from 1 cup of cider and the maple syrup. Bake at 325° for 1 hour, basting frequently.

At the end of the hour, remove ham from the oven and make diagonal cuts into the top of it. Stud the ham with raisins. Surround the ham with washed and cored apples (prepared according to the recipe that follows), over which you have dribbled some of the cider-syrup sauce. Return to oven, and cook until the apples are done.

BAKED APPLES

Core, but do not peel apples. Arrange apples in roasting pan with ham; dribble butter into holes, and sprinkle with raisins and nutmeg. When serving, a dollop of sour cream spooned on each apple makes a colorful addition to the feast.

6 baking apples
6 teaspoons melted butter
Raisins
Nutmeg
Sour cream

HORSERADISH

A lot of people don't know much about horseradish except that it is often an ingredient in seafood cocktail sauce. What a pity! Horseradish is an entity all its own, easy to grow and easy to use. You may have passed a display of horseradish at the farmers market and asked the vendor what it was. Horseradish looks like a long white root. Cultivate some in your backyard, or seek out a vendor and buy a good supply every month or so.

Horseradish
White vinegar
Sugar
Herb salt
Plain yogurt

To make a dish with horseradish, either grate the fresh root or buy prepared horseradish in a store. The best approach is to make your own preparation and keep it in your refrigerator for when the mood hits.

Clean the root well and scrape the skin off the outside of the root. Wash again. You may want to wear a mask; your eyes will water, your nose will run, and you will understand that horseradish is serious stuff.

Cut horseradish root into small chunks, and put into a blender set at medium speed. Add enough white vinegar to make a paste-like mixture. Per cup of paste, add 1 tablespoon sugar, ½ cup plain yogurt, and herb salt, to taste.

Store in your refrigerator in a tightly closed jar. The paste will keep for only a couple of weeks, and will give you a chance to try horseradish as a garnish for meats, cheeses, and anything that needs a little kick.

CAPELLINI WITH MEAT SAUCE

Capellini is the pasta of the gods. It is whisper-thin vermicelli that melts in your mouth—almost as if you're eating nothing, but with a delicate egg and butter taste. Search the Italian stands until you find it, and then buy lots. My introduction to capellini was with a tomato meat sauce. Use fresh, peeled summer tomatoes if they're available; if not, use canned Italian tomatoes.

Sauté chopped onion and minced garlic in olive oil and butter. Add diced celery and carrots. Stir vegetables as they cook.

In a heavy saucepan, cook hamburger and Italian sausages. Break the sausage skins open and remove. Break up the sausage meat, and make sure that it mixes well with the hamburger.

Drain the fat from the meat. Add the meat to the vegetables and stir. Then add tomatoes, tomato paste, and one can filled with red wine. Add a pinch of sugar and stir everything together. Reduce heat to simmer, cover, and leave the pot alone for a half hour or so. Just before serving, sprinkle with oregano.

Serve the meat sauce on the capellini, with freshly grated Parmesan cheese. Spaghetti will never be the same again.

Capellini
2 tablespoons olive oil
2 tablespoons butter
1 medium-sized onion, chopped
2 cloves garlic, minced
¼ cup diced celery
¼ cup diced carrots
½ pound lean hamburger
½ pound mild Italian sausage
4 fresh tomatoes, diced or 1 large can Italian tomatoes
1 6-ounce can tomato paste
1 tomato paste can-full red wine
Pinch of sugar
Oregano
Parmesan cheese, freshly grated

PESTO FOR PASTA

Pesto is almost a garnish. It is wonderful on pasta—second only to linguini with clam sauce. But experiment with it—have it on pasta, but also spread it on garlic toast for hors d'oeuvres, or use it as a stuffing for lamb chops or a sauce for poached eggs.

Put the garlic, pignoli nuts and basil in the blender. Gradually add the olive oil until the mixture is well blended. Add cheese and blend for a few seconds.

If you are serving pesto with pasta, cook the pasta al dente, and then drain quickly and lay pasta on a serving platter. Add steamed vegetables of your choice—tiny diced carrots and broccoli work well. Put butter on top of pasta and work in with forks. You can sprinkle the pasta with a little fine-chopped parsley, but serve the pesto sauce separately. Eat immediately, then run back to the kitchen and make some more.

2 cloves garlic, peeled and halved

½ cup olive oil

Lots of fresh basil leaves (a cup or more)

½ cup Parmesan cheese, freshly grated

½ cup pignoli nuts (pine nuts)

3 tablespoons butter, for pasta

PASTA BUFFET

You can have a lot of fun with food, and have a lot of fun at the market if you plan a pasta buffet for a party dinner. Go to the fresh pasta stand, and buy several kinds and widths of pasta. You will need several pots of boiling water to cook the pasta, and several people to help to make sure that the pasta does not overcook. If you can, get your guests into the kitchen, and have them "order" their favorite kind of pasta and how they want it cooked. Then have them proceed to the table.

   On the table, arrange platters and bowls of pasta toppings for your guests to pick and choose and combine as they will. Have chunks of fresh Parmesan cheese with graters placed in strategic locations on the table. Also, generous shakers of oregano, dried basil, and a small dish of minced garlic will be appreciated. You'll be amazed at some of the combinations . . . and at how good they taste!

*Mussels sautéed in butter
   and wine*
Sautéed Chinese pea pods
Crumbled bacon slices
Stewed tomatoes
Sautéed mushrooms
Strips of prosciutto ham
Pesto sauce (see recipe)
Avocado purée (see recipe)

PEANUT BUTTER AND CHOCOLATE SWEET TREATS

In a large mixing bowl, mix main ingredients together with your fingers. Shape the mixture into balls by rolling teaspoonfuls of it between the palms of your hands. Roll the candies in sesame seeds and sunflower seeds that have been ground up or hammered between two pieces of wax paper.

Lay the candies on sheets of wax paper with a protective layer of wax paper on top, and refrigerate for about 3 hours before serving. Put candy on a plate and have Halloween trick or treaters help themselves!

1 *cup peanut butter*
1 *cup honey*
½ *cup chocolate chips (semisweet)*
¼ *cup ground coconut*
¼ *cup non-fat instant dry milk*

Coating
Pulverized sesame seeds and sunflower seeds

NOVEMBER

Carrot Chowder	Baked Eggs Florentine
Hot Potato Salad	Whole Vegetable Tempura
Pickled Eggs	Jerusalem Artichokes with
Veal Tarragon	Pignoli Nuts
★ Thanksgiving Buffet ★	Pumpkin Pie with Ice Cream
Roast Stuffed Turkey with	East Barnard Cracker Pudding
Sausage-Mushroom Dressing	Pumpkin Face Cookies
Curried Corn Pudding	Apple Granola Layered Dessert
	Hollywood Cider

CARROT CHOWDER

If you are buying carrots, try to get the winter varieties, which are recognizable as a little fatter and less long than the Bugs Bunny type of carrots that come in plastic bags. They'll be rounder on the ends, too.

Actually, it doesn't really matter what type of carrots you use; just make sure that there is enough meat on the carrot to provide a good quantity of carrot. One winter carrot can have as much meat as two "perfect" carrots—keep that in mind when you shop for carrots.

Sauté diced carrots and celery ribs in a heavy skillet with the olive oil. When they begin to soften, move them to a large, heavy saucepan. Stir for a minute, and then add chicken broth and rosemary. Turn the heat up to high, and bring the whole pot to a boil. Then remove the pot from heat and let it cool in a cold water bath or at room temperature. Next pour the soup by batches into an electric blender, and blend at medium or "purée" speed. Return soup to saucepan and heat slowly over low heat.

Add the egg to the heavy cream and beat well, but do not whip the cream. You just want it to be thick. Add egg-cream mixture to the saucepan and fold in slowly. Keep heat on low and stir until everything is uniform.

Pour into serving dishes or serve in a big cauldron or tureen. Garnish the top of the serving dishes with slices of hard-boiled egg and sprigs of fresh parsley.

Leftovers can be gently reheated in the top of a doubleboiler.

8 *cleaned, peeled and diced carrots*
2 *tablespoons olive oil*
2 *celery stalks, peeled and diced*
1 *quart chicken broth*
1 *teaspoon dried rosemary*
1 *cup heavy cream*
1 *egg, beaten*
Fresh parsley sprigs
Hard-boiled egg slices

HOT POTATO SALAD

Boil the potato cubes in a pan of water so that potatoes are covered. Cook for 20 minutes or until tender.

In a heavy frying pan, fry the bacon until done. Remove from pan and drain on paper towels. Reduce heat to medium and add garlic and onion to the pan. Toss the garlic and onion until they are coated with the bacon grease and then sauté them, stirring often, until they become tender and golden. Add peas and sauté enough to coat with grease.

Stir in the vinegar, and crack the eggs and let them drop into the pan. Stir the egg around, scrambling it as you go.

Add drained potato cubes to contents of pan. Fold ingredients together, being careful to keep potatoes from breaking. Then add zucchini and carrot and cook all, omelet-style, making sure that everything is mixed together well.

When eggs are set, fold in sour cream and mix well with all ingredients. Turn out into a serving dish and garnish with lemon wedges and top with grated Parmesan cheese. Crumble bacon over all.

6 *potatoes, peeled and cubed*
3 *slices lean bacon*
1 *onion, minced*
1 *clove garlic, minced*
1 *cup snow peas*
½ *cup cider vinegar*
2 *eggs*
1 *cup sour cream*
⅓ *cup grated zucchini*
⅓ *cup grated carrot*
Lemon wedges
Grated Parmesan cheese

PICKLED EGGS

No self-respecting barroom would be caught without a jar of pickled eggs on the bar, and if you work in one, sooner or later you're going to learn how to like them. And somebody's got to make them, too. Once you learn to like them, you'll find yourself making them by the gallon jar and giving them to people for gifts. Or open your own honky-tonk. You've got a good start.

Lay the gallon glass jar of your choice on its side on the kitchen counter. Peel each egg and put it in the jar. You may need more than a dozen to fill the jar—it depends on the size and shape of your jar and the size of your eggs. The other ingredients will do for any number of eggs.

In a saucepan, combine all the other ingredients and simmer over medium heat, stirring occasionally to mix things up a little. Stir and cook for about 5 minutes. Remove from heat and let cool a bit. Turn the jar upright and pour the mixture (which should be hot but not boiling) over the eggs. Tamp down the onions a little bit, so they get distributed through the jar.

Put the eggs in the back of the refrigerator for 2 to 3 days, then bring them out and call all your friends. Always serve with a salt and a pepper shaker for each eater. For fun, serve bar style with just a napkin, no plate, and see how your guests react. Somebody ought to invent an egg holder for snack eating, but that would take all the challenge out of these slippery little devils.

12 *hard-boiled large eggs*
2 *cups white vinegar*
1 *large onion, sliced in thin rings*
3 *cloves of garlic, cut up*
4 *tablespoons superfine white sugar*
1 *teaspoon salt*
2½ *teaspoons dill weed*
10 *black peppercorns*

VEAL TARRAGON

Remove veal roast from wrapping and let sit at room temperature while you prepare seasoning. Preheat oven to 325°. Place roast in a roasting pan with a flat bottom.

    With a mortar and pestle or with a blender on low speed, mix lemon peel, tarragon, salt, and garlic together. Ingredients will soften and mix together, although lemon peel may be tough enough to call for the addition of a few drops of olive oil. The consistency should be paste-like when you are through. If your mix is too liquid because of added oil, add some dried parsley to soak up liquid. It won't affect the taste much.

    When you are satisfied with your paste, transfer it to a small bowl. With a large, sharp chef's knife, make slits about half an inch deep in the face of the roast. You may wish to make slits going at 45-degree angles to one another for maximum flavoring, but a series of parallel slits the length of the roast will do just fine. Pack each slit full of the flavoring paste by spreading slit open with fork and a sharp knife. You will get a wedge-like effect.

    Place roast in the middle of the oven on a rack and roast for about 2 hours, or until done to your liking. You may baste occasionally. Reserve pan juices for a flavoring sauce for vegetables.

3–4 *pound veal roast*
Peel of ½ fresh lemon
2 *teaspoons fresh tarragon*
2 *teaspoons salt*
1 *clove garlic, peeled*
Few drops of oil

THANKSGIVING BUFFET

Holidays can be tough. The pressures can be intense, whether you're entertaining and feeding a hungry crowd of relatives or deciding what to do if you're alone. The way I figure it, holidays should be spent with people you like. And to some people, a holiday spent alone is a disaster. So I like to call up friends who don't have family nearby and put them all together for a buffet dinner. In the spring, it's an ecumenical "Eastover Feastover" and for Thanksgiving, it's the "Big Bird Buffet." If you've had it with Aunt Gertrude, come to my house next year for Thanksgiving. We'll all be there.

The Menu

Roast, Stuffed Turkey with Sausage-Mushroom Dressing
Curried Corn Pudding
Baked Eggs Florentine
Whole-Vegetable Tempura
Jerusalem Artichokes with Pignoli Nuts
Pumpkin Pie with Vanilla Ice Cream
East Barnard Cracker Pudding

ROAST STUFFED TURKEY WITH SAUSAGE–MUSHROOM DRESSING

Prepare the stuffing ahead of time. Fry the sausage and onion together until the onion begins to brown. Add 2 tablespoons of butter and let it melt in the pan. Then add the sliced mushrooms and cook everything together, stirring gently, until the mushrooms are limp and buttery.

In a large mixing bowl combine bread crumbs, chestnuts, celery, parsley, and seasonings. When well mixed, add the sausage mixture. Then stir in egg and sherry and mix until everything is moist. Add more sherry if necessary.

Rinse the turkey inside and out and pat dry with paper towels. Singe the outside of the turkey with a match to remove any clinging feathers. Stuff the dressing into the body and neck cavities, being careful not to pack it too tightly. If you like, truss the breast of the

1 12-pound turkey
Lots of butter
¼ cup white flour
Salt, pepper

ROAST STUFFED TURKEY, *continued*

turkey to hold the stuffing in place. I just tuck the neck skin and breast skin over the bird and hope that it all stays in place. It usually does.

Place the stuffed bird on a rack in a large roasting pan in a 400° oven. Brush melted butter over the whole breast and sprinkle flour on the breast area. The bird will roast quickly.

When the flour starts to turn brown, reduce the heat to 325°. Mix together five tablespoons of melted butter and ⅔ cup white wine. Season the turkey with this basting mixture. Just pour it into the base of the pan with the turkey juices and use a squeeze-bulb baster. Sprinkle salt and pepper lightly over the turkey.

Baste the turkey every 15 minutes. If the skin seems to be getting too brown and crackly, put an aluminum foil tent over the whole bird.

Roast an hour for every 3 pounds of turkey. The bird is done when you wiggle a drumstick and it falls off into your hand. Remove the bird from oven and allow to cool for 20 minutes before slicing. Serve dressing separately.

Stuffing

1½ cups stale coarse bread crumbs
Butter
1 cup cooked chestnuts, chopped
1 pound mild Italian sausage meat
1 onion, diced
1 stalk of celery, diced
2 cups sliced mushrooms
2 tablespoons dried parsley flakes
Salt, pepper
2 teaspoons sage
4 tablespoons sherry
2 eggs, well beaten

Basting mixture

5 tablespoons melted butter
⅔ cup white wine

CURRIED CORN PUDDING

Melt the butter in a medium-sized skillet. Add green pepper and onion, and sauté slowly until soft. Then stir in the curry powder until pepper and onion are well coated.

In a large mixing bowl, add cream to the corn. Stir in the eggs, salt, and sugar. Next stir in the pepper-and-onion mixture and mix thoroughly.

Pour mixture into a well buttered 1¼-quart soufflé dish. Bake at 350° for 45 minutes or until puffy and slightly browned on top.

½ cup minced onion
½ cup minced green pepper
3 tablespoons butter
1 tablespoon curry powder
2 cups cooked corn kernels
2 cups light cream
3 eggs, lightly beaten
1 teaspoon salt
½ teaspoon sugar

BAKED EGGS FLORENTINE

Besides being great at Thanksgiving, this dish is a perennial favorite at the one brunch a year I get up in time to attend. It's easy to make and yet people will think that you rose at dawn to start assembling it. Just boil the eggs the night before and sleep as late as you want.

Preheat the oven to 250°. Melt 3 tablespoons of the butter in a wide skillet. Add salt, pepper, and nutmeg, along with spinach. Stir the spinach, coating it with butter and flavorings. Cook until the spinach shrinks up and lumps together, about 5 minutes. Move the spinach to one side, squeezing it with the back of a wooden spoon to get all the liquid out. Let the liquid cook out by tilting the pan so the liquid runs into the center. When liquid is just about all gone, remove spinach from heat.

In another pan, melt 4 tablespoons of butter and sauté the onion. Stir it constantly with a wooden spoon so that it does not brown. Sprinkle onion with flour to thicken. Cook until bubbly.

Stir in hot milk to make a smooth sauce for the onions, which will float in the sauce. When the sauce starts to bubble, remove from heat. Stir in the Jarlsberg cheese.

Add half the cream mixture to the spinach mixture. Fold until the spinach is well distributed throughout the sauce.

Lay this spinach-cheese mixture on the bottom of a buttered 8-cup casserole dish. Lay the quartered eggs in a colorful pattern on top of the spinach. Pour the rest of the cheese sauce over the eggs. Bake at 250° for about 10 minutes. Don't overcook or the eggs will get rubbery.

7 tablespoons butter
½ teaspoon salt
Dash of pepper
Dash of nutmeg
1 pound fresh, clean, trimmed spinach
1 medium onion, chopped
3 tablespoons flour
2 cups hot milk
½ cup shredded Jarlsberg cheese
12 hard-boiled eggs, quartered

WHOLE-VEGETABLE TEMPURA

This type of tempura is for those who like their vegetables crunchy on the inside and golden crusted on the outside. Use spears of broccoli, tiny zucchini, tiny eggplants, whole small carrots, and whole onions. You can also use squash blossoms and pumpkin blossoms in this recipe. Whatever you use is apt to taste just fine. Just remember that this style of cooking requires your constant attention.

2 eggs
1 cup water
½ teaspoon salt
Flour
Vegetable oil for frying
Variety of seasonal vegetables

Wash and peel the vegetables, if necessary, and pat dry with paper towels. Pour about 1 inch of vegetable oil into a heavy skillet and heat steadily over medium-high heat.

Mix together the eggs and water. Add salt and mix again. Make sure that the egg is well beaten, no streaks of dark and light yellow. Add enough flour to make a thin batter that drips easily off the end of a wooden spoon.

Plunge each vegetable into the batter and roll until completely covered. Pull the vegetable out and let a few drops stream back into the bowl. Then pop the vegetable into the hot oil, which will sizzle when the vegetable touches it.

Cook only a few vegetables at a time, making sure that the oil temperature won't drop too much. When a thick golden crust has formed around the vegetable on all sides, remove from the oil and drain on paper towels. Try to serve immediately; but if you can't, try to keep them warm in an oven, wrapped inside dish towels or napkins.

Serve with lemon and light soy sauce.

JERUSALEM ARTICHOKES WITH PIGNOLI NUTS

Peel the artichokes. Wash under running water and, if they are large, cut them up into uniform-sized pieces. Cover with cold water in a large kettle and bring to a boil, with a cover on the pan. Boil for 5 minutes, covered. Then drain off all the water and rinse the artichokes with cold water.

Heat the oil and butter in a large frying pan. Add the garlic and let it fry for a minute or two. Then add the drained artichokes. Cook, stirring, over medium heat for about 5 minutes. Then sprinkle with the pinch of sugar, and salt and pepper to taste. Stir to mix.

Add the pignoli nuts and sauté for 5 minutes. By then, the artichokes should be golden and coated. Sprinkle parsley over the whole panful, and stir once to distribute. Transfer contents to serving dish.

2 pounds Jerusalem artichokes
Salt and pepper
2 tablespoons vegetable oil
4 tablespoons butter
Pinch of sugar
1 clove garlic, minced
Handful fresh parsley leaves
1 cup pignoli nuts, finely chopped

PUMPKIN PIE WITH VANILLA ICE CREAM

Prepare a 9-inch pastry pie shell. Prick the bottom with a fork. Bake the pumpkin halves in a 350° oven until they are soft. Scrape the meat from the skin and measure 2 cups of meat, mashed. Put the pumpkin meat in a big mixing bowl with the cup of hot (not boiling) milk, and the eggs, sugar, ginger, and cinnamon. Mix everything together well and pour into the pie shell.

Sprinkle a little extra nutmeg on top of the pie. Bake for 35 to 40 minutes at 350°, and test with a knife. When the knife comes out clean, the pie is done.

1 9-inch pie crust
1 sugar pumpkin, cut in half
1 cup hot milk
2 eggs, beaten
½ cup sugar
½ teaspoon ginger
½ teaspoon cinnamon

EAST BARNARD CRACKER PUDDING

East Barnard, Vermont is quite a place and this is quite a dessert. It was passed on to me by JoJo Levasseur, one of the Leavitt family members who inhabit the Broad Brook Valley, in which East Barnard nestles. It sounds plain. Maybe it even looks plain. But it's sort of like East Barnard—a lot more than meets the eye.

Unwrap the saltines and break, don't crumble them. Mix together the sugar, eggs, and milk. Add to crackers. Cook all in a saucepan over low heat until thick. Do not stir. It should take 30 to 60 minutes to thicken; then remove the pudding from heat and pour into serving bowl.

Boil 1¾ cups of water. Mix ¼ cup of cold water with the cornstarch until it is smooth. Add to the boiling water, with sugar and salt.

Let this mixture boil for about five minutes; then take it off the heat, and add butter, lemon juice, and a little bit of nutmeg. Stir until the butter melts. Then pour over the cracker pudding.

You can hear a hundred contented sighs rise over the valley on Thanksgiving afternoon as this is served.

2 stacks of wrapped saltines
1 cup sugar
2 eggs
2 quarts (or less) whole milk

Sauce

1 cup sugar
2 tablespoons cornstarch
2 cups boiling water
Salt
6 tablespoons butter
3 teaspoons lemon juice
Nutmeg

PUMPKIN FACE COOKIES

Combine filling ingredients; cook and stir until bubbly and smooth. Cool mixture while making cookie dough.

Cream shortening and sugar. Beat in egg and molasses. Place oats in blender and chop finely. Mix oats, flour, baking soda, and salt, and stir into creamed mixture. Cover and chill for 1 hour.

On a floured board, roll dough ⅛ inch thick. Cut dough into 36 3-inch circles. On 18 of the circles, place a teaspoon of the pumpkin filling. Cut faces in remaining circles. Place cut faces on top of filled circles. Seal edges. Press stems from scraps of dough. Bake on greased cookie sheet at 375° for 12 minutes.

Pumpkin filling

½ cup cooked mashed pumpkin
½ cup sugar
½ teaspoon cinnamon
½ teaspoon nutmeg
½ teaspoon ginger

Cookie dough

¾ cup butter or margarine
1 egg
¼ cup light molasses
1 teaspoon salt
½ cup light brown sugar
2 cups flour
½ teaspoon baking soda
1 cup quick cooking oats

APPLE GRANOLA LAYERED DESSERT

Butter an 8-inch square glass baking dish and put a layer of grain down on the bottom of the dish (about ⅓ of the 2 cups). Top this layer with a layer of sliced apples. Sprinkle a little bit of lemon juice on the apples to prevent discoloration. Then sprinkle half the brown sugar and a shake of cinnamon on apples. Put dabs of butter on top. Then start again with a layer of grain; a layer of apples; and a layer of brown sugar, cinnamon and butter. Top with a last layer of grain and butter tabs. Bake at 350° for 1 hour. Serve very hot, with very cold vanilla ice cream. Pour warmed maple syrup over all.

2 cups commercial or homemade grain mixture (granola, Quaker 100% Natural cereal, Familia)
2 cups peeled and sliced tart apples
1 teaspoon lemon juice
½ cup brown sugar
1 teaspoon cinnamon
2 tablespoons butter
Vanilla ice cream
Maple syrup

HOLLYWOOD CIDER

Heat two gallons of cider *gently* in a large, heavy stockpot. Add four to six cinnamon sticks for flavoring, according to what your personal taste may be.

Arrange drink glasses on a serving tray. Glass mugs are the perfect serving glasses for this drink.

When the cider is steaming, remove the pan from the heat. Uncork a bottle of champagne and have it ready. Enlist the aid of an assistant.

Ladle the cider into each glass. Fill each glass two-thirds full with cider. Assistant should follow behind you and fill each glass to the rim with champagne. Open additional bottles of champagne as you need them.

This drink can be made cold and served as a punch at a buffet or cocktail party. Just remember the proportion of two gallons of cider to one quart of champagne. If your budget allows and you feel extravagant, up the champagne to half-and-half—no one will complain. To serve as a punch, just mix together immediately before serving. Make sure that both liquids are well-chilled.

2 gallons of sweet cider
1 quart champagne
Handful of cinnamon sticks

DECEMBER

★Breakfast Specialty Treats★
Glazed Apples and Ham
Apple Flapjacks
Farmers Cheese for Breakfast
Mimosa Cocktail for Brunch
★Food Stamps Go to Market★
Oyster Stew
★Gingerbread House★

Sculpture Dough
Your Christmas Goose
Sesame Pie Crust
Banana Ricotta Pie
★Attracting the Elderly★
Office Party Eggnog
Liptauer Cheese Spread
Banana Rum Cocktail
Jamaican Coffee

W. DAVID POWELL 1982

SOME BREAKFAST SPECIALTY TREATS

1. Make a dip of 4 ounces cream cheese and ¼ cup plain yogurt. Sprinkle cinnamon sugar on top and serve with hulled, washed strawberries.

2. Slice a loaf of whole wheat bread. Lay thick slices of cheddar cheese on each slice and top with sliced apples. Put under the broiler until the cheese softens but does not quite melt.

3. Serve baking powder biscuits split open and filled with fresh strawberry preserves and cream cheese.

GLAZED APPLES AND HAM

In a skillet, mix together honey, butter and mustard. Heat slowly.

Add ham and apples, and cook on low heat. When coated with glaze and heated through, transfer ham and apples to a platter. Serve with scrambled eggs.

1 cup honey
2 tablespoons butter
1 tablespoon Pommery mustard
1 pound sliced baked ham
2 large apples, sliced

APPLE FLAPJACKS

In a large mixing bowl, combine eggs and sugar. Add milk, flour, and baking powder and stir together. Add apples and mix well.

Melt a tablespoon of butter in a frying pan and adjust heat. Drop in pancake batter by spoonfuls, and flip when underside is brown. You can tell when a pancake is ready to flip from the first side; air bubbles will form on the uncooked surface. Flip each pancake over, and remove from pan when second side is brown.

Sprinkle the pancakes with cinnamon sugar and pour melted butter and maple syrup over them. Garnish with a slice of red-skinned apple.

1 large apple, peeled and cubed
3 eggs
½ cup sugar
1 cup milk
¾ cup flour
1 teaspoon baking powder
Butter for frying
Maple syrup
Cinnamon sugar

FARMERS CHEESE FOR BREAKFAST

If you're going to buy farmers cheese, look for tubs of fresh farmers cheese at a deli-type farm stand. Do not buy the prepackaged kind unless you can read the package carefully to see what additives were thrown in to keep the color white and the mass perfect. Potassium sorbate is a common additive to farmers cheese.

Farmers cheese
Melted butter

There's not much difference between farmers cheese and cottage cheese except that farmers cheese has been pressed into a block that is easy to slice.

For breakfast, allow one slice per person. Preheat oven to 250°. Coat bottom and sides of a shallow baking dish or pie plate with melted butter. Lay the slices on the buttered surface and dribble a little bit of butter over the slices.

Cook until the slices turn lightly golden and a small crust of butter starts to form.

MIMOSA COCKTAIL FOR BRUNCH

The Mimosa has become pretty standard fare at home brunches although the Bloody Mary is still popular. Mimosa is pretty innocuous punch; even nondrinkers will enjoy it. It is so innocuous, though, that the host would be wise to remind guests that it is alcoholic.

2 quarts champagne
1 quart fresh orange juice
Grenadine syrup

To make a party-sized bowl of Mimosa, pour 2 quarts of champagne and one quart of fresh orange juice into a large punch bowl. Use that ratio (2:1) for refills, also. For added color, make frozen cubes of grenadine syrup and water (1 tablespoon per ice tray).

FOOD STAMPS GO TO MARKET

Redeeming food stamps is another way of attracting business. It sounds complicated to apply for a redemption license, but once the initial paperwork is done, the added business will outweigh the hassle.

For food stamps, the first decision should be whether individual vendors should apply for licenses or whether the market as a whole should apply. The answer depends on the structure of the market. If the market is owned and operated cooperatively, the coop should apply. But if the alliance is loose, let individual vendors apply and then hang out a shingle advertising their licenses. And let the public—especially local social welfare workers—know that the market is taking food stamps. The word will get around.

To apply for your redemption license, contact your regional office of the U.S. Department of Agriculture's Food and Nutrition Service. Ask for a retailer's application form. Read the pamphlet that explains the process before you fill out the application. The application is followed up by an appointment with a reviewer from the Food Stamp Program, who will give the applicant a little quiz about food stamp transactions and ask questions about the set-up of the market.

OYSTER STEW

This stew has no exotic ingredients and no detailed directions. Just remember to reserve the liquid that is in the container of oysters. If you forget or if there is not enough, add dry vermouth.

Put 1 cup of the oyster liquid in a saucepan with the oysters. Heat gently, and cook the oysters until the sides curl up. Drain off the liquid and reserve the oysters.

Meanwhile, heat the other cup of liquid in a soup kettle. When it starts to boil, skim the foam off the top. Add the cream, butter, a dash of celery salt, and pepper.

When the ingredients are thoroughly heated (don't let them boil, for the cream will curdle) slip in the oysters. If the oysters have gotten cold, let them reheat gently in the stew. If they are still warm, serve stew immediately with fresh bread. Garnish with watercress.

1 *quart shucked oysters*
2 *cups oyster liquid*
2 *cups heavy cream*
4 *tablespoons butter*
Celery salt
Pepper

GINGERBREAD HOUSE

The most beautiful gingerbread house I ever saw was made by Margaret Hanni. Obviously Margaret had worked for days, maybe even weeks, on this architectural masterpiece. It was ensconced on a table of its own at a restaurant employees' Christmas party, but had been on display for restaurant customers. I didn't know Margaret at the time; I only knew that she was the woman who had made the gingerbread house. But I got to know her that night. One of my best friendships started on a very bad note.

You can blame it on Chuck Berry, you can blame it on the champagne, or you can blame it on my charming dance partner. But in the middle of "Nadine" ("Nadine . . . why can't you be true?")

we did a jitterbug roll, and suddenly, I was airborne. When I came down, my partner and I were on top of the gingerbread house. On the floor. The Marx Brothers couldn't have done it any better. Our faces were covered with frosting. The south wall clung to my hand. And Margaret was in tears.

That night, I learned how to make a gingerbread house—or at least an imitation that would promise to be jitterbug-proof. My friend Roger and I found a recipe for cement-like sculpture dough, and began to build a dream house. Since then, I've made many; and I use the same recipe for making dough ornaments and decorations for Christmas. Try it. It's inedible (unless you like salt dough), but it's lots of fun.

SCULPTURE DOUGH

Add water slowly to flour and salt. Mix well with your hands and then turn out on a floured board. Knead with your hands for about five minutes, then roll it out to a thickness of about 1 inch or so, depending on what you are going to use it for. Get a sharp paring knife and have a pan of boiling water on the stove.

1½ cups water
4 cups flour
1 cup salt

Make the walls of the house by trimming the rolled out dough into walls shapes. Use glasses, vases, or anything that you have around for cookie-cutter-type punching out for windows and doors.

Lay your finished walls and roof on a greased baking sheet. Bake at 350° for 45 minutes or more. Test with a pin. When it comes out clean, they are done. Bake other house parts. Cool.

Assemble your house with glue and then shellac. Paint first, if desired.

For decoration, put some dough into a garlic press, and press through to make textured patterns. Be sure to rinse the press out in very hot water as soon as you are done.

YOUR CHRISTMAS GOOSE

When it comes to goose, think ahead. You may have a hard time finding a goose to cook. It may be necessary to order one to insure a fresh bird. If you can't find a fresh bird, you can usually order a frozen one, or maybe even buy a frozen one at a gourmet specialty shop. Serving portions are about the same as for turkey. This recipe will do for a 12-pound goose.

If the goose is frozen, allow it two or three days to thaw in your refrigerator. The day before you are to serve it, lay it on a rack, wrapper removed, and pierce the breast with a sharp fork to allow some of the fat to drain off.

If you have a fresh goose, wash it inside and out and singe off any tiny feathers with a lit match rubbed along the skin surface. Then pierce the breast with a fork, as above, and let it drain for an hour or more before roasting.

For a stuffed goose combine stuffing ingredients in a large mixing bowl. Stuff this mixture loosely into the goose's body cavity, and truss.

Put the goose in a roasting pan, and bake at 400° for 2½ to 3 hours. As it roasts, baste often with a mixture of one-half apple cider and one-half dark beer.

As the goose browns, keep an eye on it. When the skin starts to look papery, lay a shallow dish of water in the oven; the steam will prevent the goose from getting too dry. Don't let the water pan dry out.

The goose is done when a long fork pierced through the breast shows clear juices instead of pink juices. For a finishing touch, pour melted butter over the bird and increase oven temperature to 500°. Remove bird when skin reaches desired color and texture.

Let the goose sit for about 15 minutes before carving.

12-pound goose
Apple cider
Dark beer
Melted butter

Stuffing

4 *cups chopped tart apples*
4 *cups stale bread crumbs*
½ *cup diced celery*
1 *teaspoon sage*
Enough milk to moisten
    ingredients

SESAME PIE CRUST

Combine flour, sesame seeds, and powdered sugar. Cut in butter. Add enough cold water to make everything stick together. This crust is especially good for exotic pies like almond cream or banana ricotta pie.

1¾ cup flour
½ cup sesame seeds
2 tablespoons powdered sugar
¾ cup butter
Cold water

BANANA RICOTTA PIE

Fill pie crust with sliced bananas. Mix together eggs, sugar, ricotta cheese, cinnamon, and nutmeg and pour over bananas.

Place pie in the center of a preheated 425° oven and bake for 10 minutes. Reduce heat to 350°, and bake for 20 more minutes or until the liquid is set. Cool. Sprinkle with powdered sugar, and serve.

9 -inch uncooked pie crust
Sliced bananas
3 large eggs
¾ cup sugar or honey
1 pound ricotta cheese
1 teaspoon cinnamon
½ teaspoon nutmeg
Confectioners' sugar

ATTRACTING THE ELDERLY

The farmers markets can compete with supermarkets for the buyer's business. Using France as an example again, the Paris farmers market is centrally located. Elderly people especially enjoy shopping there, and many do so every day. The result is that their nutrition is improved by the wealth of fresh foods available.

Elderly people may not be able to get transportation to supermarkets, which tend to be located on highways far from their neighborhoods. The markets can also provide them with a daily walk and some social interaction. They can buy just enough for a day or two and not be burdened by heavy shopping bags.

Make sure that your farmers market is publicized through the local senior citizens' groups and welfare agencies. Perhaps you might offer a discount to senior citizens to attract their business. Or publish a cookbook for senior citizens, on how to cook fresh food for just one or two people.

OFFICE PARTY EGGNOG

People who have jobs have office parties, but the rest of us, the freelancers of the world, have no one to chase around offices and can't afford lampshades to wear on our heads. In my time, I have attended a few "office parties" for client companies, and most were held in fancy restaurants with employees in chiffon and stiff shirts. They were a far cry from the office parties that the *Playboy* cartoons depict. So I thought I would change all that by having an office party at Christmas for my freelance friends. Now it's a tradition, so I've got to keep it up; the invitation ends with "Bring your own office." If office parties were only what they used to be, they'd make this eggnog. We make it at ours. Bring back office parties!

1 dozen large eggs
2½ cups white sugar
Half-gallon milk
1 pint Kahlua liqueur
1 quart Saronno Amaretto liqueur
Pinch of salt
Fresh nutmeg
Vanilla bean
½ cup slivered almonds

Separate eggs into separate bowls. With a wire whisk, beat the egg yolks together. Add half a cup of the sugar, stirring as you add. Beat the egg yolks again to make sure that they are well mixed. Then slowly pour in the half gallon of milk and mix well again. Open liqueur bottles and slowly add both liquids to the mix and give a few good strong stirs with the whisk. Then cover the bowl with plastic wrap and set it out on the porch, or somewhere else cool and undisturbed.

With a hand or electric beater, whip the egg whites, adding a pinch of salt as you whip. When the whites form stiff peaks, they are ready. Stop beating, and slowly fold in one cup of sugar. Beat to form peaks again.

In a third bowl, whip the cream until it is stiff. Then carefully transfer the whipped cream to the base of the serving bowl, preferably a large punch bowl with a ladle. Or, you may wish to be creative and use a pastry cloth. Squeeze the whipped cream in a spiral pattern around the sides of the bowl.

OFFICE PARTY EGGNOG, *continued*

Back in the first bowl, uncover and fold in egg whites. Pour entire contents, well-stirred, into serving bowl over the whipped cream. Stir gently, if you must. Grate nutmeg over top of bowl and sprinkle slivered almonds or adorn with a single vanilla bean.

You can also just serve the egg whites–egg yolks mixture in the serving bowl and portion out the whipped cream in the base of serving glasses. This is quite elegant, but you'd better remember to serve some sort of stirrer. It will stand up straight in the glass—kind of nice.

LIPTAUER CHEESE SPREAD

Garlic lovers unite! Spread some of this wonderful, garlicky cheese on dark bread and go into orbit.

Cream together all ingredients except the spices. You'll need a good strong wooden spoon and a flat-bottomed bowl to get this done with any efficiency. When you have something that looks pretty uniform in color except for the bits of olive and carrot, begin to add the spices.

Mix all together again to make sure that spices get integrated. Then form into a large mound, and put on a platter for serving or stuff into a container to keep in the refrigerator.

1 pound cream cheese
2 tablespoons unsalted butter
⅓ cup grated Cheddar cheese
⅓ cup grated Parmesan cheese
⅓ cup grated Mozzarella cheese
¼ cup chopped onion
3 tablespoons diced green olives
⅓ cup grated carrots
1 tablespoon minced garlic
Dash of dried thyme
1 teaspoon fresh dill
1 teaspoon paprika
Salt and pepper to taste

BANANA RUM COCKTAIL

There's more to this drink than meets the eye—or taste buds. It tastes like dessert, but if you drink a couple you won't be able to find your way home. Proceed with caution, but enjoy with delight.

    For two drinks: Pour everything into the blender and blend at medium speed until the banana breaks up. Keep blending until you see a uniform color. If it is too thick, add some ice cubes.

    Pour into brandy snifters and garnish with a wedge of fresh lime and a dash of nutmeg.

1 banana
1 scoop vanilla ice cream
½ cup Tia Maria liqueur
¾ cup dark rum
¾ cup milk
Dash of lime juice

JAMAICAN COFFEE

Cut up the lime and use the quarters to moisten the rim of a large brandy snifter. Then pour a little bit of sugar onto a barside cutting board and turn the glass so that the rim side slices around in the sugar and gets all coated.

    Very carefully, pour in the Grand Marnier and the Tia Maria or Kahlua. Tip the glass so that the liqueurs coat the sides but do not disturb the sugar and lime coating on the rim.

    Fill the remainder of the glass with the freshly brewed coffee, except for about ¼ inch of headspace at the mouth of the glass. Heap whipped cream in a mound in the center and work it to a small peak, again trying to avoid the lime and sugar as much as possible. Top the whipped cream with a half-teaspoon of orange juice concentrate. It should be quite grainy and will sink into the whipped cream, leaving bright color and a hint of strong orange flavor. Serve the drink with a straw.

Fresh lime, cut up
Finely granulated sugar
1 ounce Grand Marnier liqueur
1 ounce Tia Maria or Kahlua
Coffee from fresh mocha java beans
Whipped cream
Frozen orange juice concentrate

INDEX

Sunflower seed and spinach soup, 31
Swordfish, skewered, 100–1

T

Taco Madness hot sauce, 108
Tandoori chicken, 60
Tartar sauce, 27
Taylor, Dale, 21–25
Tempura, whole-vegetable, 139
Thanksgiving buffet, 136
Tomatoes
    with basil and sour cream, 96
    fried sliced, 95

Tuna, 18–19
Turkey legs, marinated barbecued, 107
Turkey, roast stuffed with sausage-mushroom dressing, 136–37

V

Veal tarragon, 135
Vinegar, lemon-mint, 85
Vinaigrette dressing, 73

W

Watermelon Eyecatcher, 89
Whipped cream topping for fresh fruit, 117
Whole vegetable tempura, 139
Wild blackberry pie, 104

Z

Zucchini bread, 88
Zucchini Mikonos, 99